CW01642482

Echoes of a Rainb... Song

With very best wishes,

Chris Curven

1999.

Echoes of a Rainbow Song

A South African Magnificat

Chris Chivers

Foreword by Imam A. Rashied Omar

The Parish of Friern Barnet · London

First Edition
published in 1996 by
Chris Chivers
St. George's Cathedral Foundation
5 Wale Street, Cape Town 8001
South Africa

Second Edition
published in 1999 by
The Parish of Friern Barnet
Friern Barnet Road, London N11 3BS
United Kingdom

ISBN 1 902908 00 7

Cover photograph:
Sunset over Table Bay
© Mary Chivers

Typeset in Lucida Handwriting
and Bookman Old Style

Printed and bound in the United Kingdom
by Thorne Printing, London

Contents

Foreword

When I was approached by Chris Chivers to write this Foreword I gave him a conditional acceptance. I vividly remember saying to him "If I find it within my capabilities after I have read your manuscript I will be honoured to write it."

At home that evening I could not help feeling ambivalent. For at that time we had known each other for literally a couple of weeks and for a Muslim to be writing the Foreword for a book of meditations, which seeks to capture the new South Africa through the eyes of a committed Christian, seemed to me to be far too presumptuous an undertaking.

Having read the manuscript, however, and discovering that it echoes the same Rainbow Song that I am endeavouring to sing, but with an Arabic rhythm and Islamic lyrics, I am greatly privileged to be writing this Foreword.

Chris Chivers has employed a unique method of making sense of his encounters during his six months working at one of South Africa's most renowned institutions of worship – St. George's Cathedral, Cape Town. He has used the text of a popular Christian prayer song, the *Magnificat* from Luke's Gospel, as a window into his personal experiences. As a result he has re-inspired us with regard to the efficacy of prayer, which has sadly all too often become lost in our secular world.

He has not merely succeeded in making important connections between the individual verses of the

Magnificat and the new phase of the struggle to establish a just South Africa, but more importantly he has succeeded in making these connections across cultural and religious divides. This I believe is the major strength and remarkable achievement of this book.

The book is also a painful but necessary reminder of the polychrome challenges which confront the nascent rainbow nation of South Africa – challenges which we ignore at our peril. Chris's moving acquaintances with Cape Town's street children, through his involvement with the Yizani Drop-in Centre, stand out as one of the most significant of these challenges. What were the factors which forced these children onto the streets? How can we arrest this calamity which is a breeding ground for crime and substance abuse? How do we reunite these children with their families? These and many other questions were spontaneously raised in my mind whilst reading the book. These are the very questions which should preoccupy the minds and energies of post-apartheid activists.

What gives a European Christian the audacity so vividly to depict the suffering and dehumanisation that stubbornly persists in the streets of the new South Africa? In the words of the Prophet Muhammad (peace and blessings be upon him) it is true faith. "Faith," he is reported to have declared, "is good counsel and advice." This is what I believe Chris Chivers has given in this book. He has given us a wonderful and priceless gift.

Most books reflect in some way or another the disposition of their authors. This book provides the reader with a **profound** insight into the compassionate and gentle nature of Chris Chivers. He is a sensitive human being who places high value on his relationships with others. But he is also perceptive and has the ingenious ability to recollect the minutest details of his exchanges.

His faithful recording of every occasion of fellowship with myself and other congregants of the Claremont Main Road Mosque is a testimony to his observant nature. We at the Claremont Main Road Mosque have been privileged to have been a small part of Chris's brief but enriching sojourn in South Africa. He has both learnt from our interfaith encounters and has taken them to new heights.

Thank you Chris for sharing a part of your life-journey with the rainbow children of South Africa. We are sure that this rainbow will follow you wherever God guides you.

God bless Africa – Nkosi Sikelel i'Afrika

Imam A. Rashied Omar
Cape Town
November 1996

Introduction to the First Edition

One of my theology supervisors at Cambridge once said to me that he hated systematic theology and that he couldn't do it because life was always untidy at the edges. Having deluded myself for some time into believing that I have a tidy mind I rather warm to the idea of a logical system to explicate the relationship between God and humanity but like my supervisor I don't believe that such a theology is possible. Other theology lecturers at Cambridge taught me that whatever theology I do I must at least be clear as to my methods. I fear that what follows will disappoint them too. For, in terms of method and genre, *Echoes of a Rainbow Song* is a thorough hybrid. All that I can say is that I have taken the *Magnificat* together with some of my experiences in South Africa – I could have chosen many more – and I have tried to create pictures (perhaps they are little parables) which should allow the reader the space in which to make such connections as seem to emerge from this process.

I chose to focus on the *Magnificat* for a number of reasons. Firstly, of all the Christian texts I know save for the *Lord's Prayer,* it is the one I know best – I've been singing it since I was eight! Secondly, it seems to me to contain some of the core teachings of Christianity. Thirdly, it presents an agenda for revolutionary change. So where better to sing it than in a country which has undergone such a remarkable – and largely peaceful – revolution in the last few years?

I chose the *Book of Common Prayer* version not because it's the most accurate translation of the original Greek but because it's the one most familiar to me and, I suspect, to most readers.

I also chose the title *Echoes of a Rainbow Song* for several reasons. The *Magnificat* is, as I've said, a revolutionary song. It expresses the up-ending of this world's values through the covenantal life, death and resurrection of Jesus Christ. It seemed appropriate therefore to dovetail this song with the 'rainbow' language of post-1994 South Africa which is, at least in part, based on echoes of the covenant which God made with Noah after the flood. The Rainbow symbolised a divine promise to Noah. The oft-quoted slogan 'we are the rainbow people of God' has similarly symbolised to many South Africans a sense of their promised fulfilment as a nation. The election in 1994 and the Rugby World Cup in 1995, to name but two events in recent South African history, very much focused around the 'promise-fulfilment' axis. A wicked apartheid system was being up-ended. This was surely just what the *Magnificat* had envisaged? Now the South African nation's task was to bring the sense of promise this engendered to fulfilment. It has been my great privilege to spend six months in South Africa watching just that – a nation engaged in a new 'struggle' to sustain the rainbow vision it has embraced. As a result of what I have experienced I have deliberately included the word 'echoes' in the title. For at one level echoes of the triumphant singing which was such a feature of 1994 and 1995 have surrounded me. But at another level of course that singing is fading into the distance. Indeed at times it seems to be echoing quite softly now as the harsh reality of what is still left to be done hits home.

A rainbow has a beautiful and visionary quality but it is an utterly transient thing. It emerges at the intersection between storm and sunshine – by analogy between suffering and triumph. But no sooner is it there in the sky than it is gone – conquered either by more sustained sunshine or by the reappearance of driving rain. Sunshine or rain. These are the stark alternatives which still face the 'rainbow nation'. Its vision is strong. But can it be brought to fulfilment?

This is the question which has confronted me at every turn during my stay in South Africa. I have no wish to be a prophet of doom about what I have seen in an all too brief six months. But I have perceived that an equally tortuous path to sustained justice and peace, truth and reconciliation, is inevitably succeeding the 'long walk to freedom' for all South Africa's citizens. So I have tried to reflect the fragility of that path in what I have written because that is what I have experienced in my stay here. It is also my belief that the questions being grappled with in South Africa are fundamentally the same questions faced by the whole global community of nations. In the story of the 'rainbow nation' this worldwide community hears echoes of its own hopes and aspirations. It catches a glimpse of a vision which it passionately desires to embrace. I hope therefore that readers will hear echoes of their own stories and situations, their own dreams and struggles, in the lives of the people who populate the pages which follow. If they do hear echoes of their own lives and experience that frisson of empathy which is the object of all story-telling then this book will have achieved a measure of what it set out to do.

Whilst it is not for me to dictate how this book is to be used, the reader may find it helpful to know that I did not intend these meditations to be read from cover to cover. There are strong thematic strands throughout the book but each meditation is nonetheless deliberately self-contained to encourage a measured response to individual phrases of the *Magnificat.* Indeed within a given meditation there are usually smaller units which in themselves might serve as springboards for lengthy reflection. In the end the reader must decide what suits best. I hope merely to have created a structure flexible enough to make such a decision a realistic possibility.

I shall not list the activities or events with which I have had a connection because they all appear in the meditations which follow. Needless to say I am immensely grateful to all the people who have allowed me to share in their work and who have been only too glad to answer my questions and to sharpen or correct my perceptions.

It is always invidious to thank people by name but I must express my gratitude to a number of people who have played such a crucial part in my six months here. Rowan Smith, Chris Ahrends, Christian Hartnick and Vivien Harber are all on the staff of St. George's Cathedral. They have greatly enriched my vision of ministry through their kindness and encouragement. Barry Smith, Michael Keall, Rowan Smith and Alan Lindhorst have provided me with beautiful homes in which to live. I am greatly indebted to them for the generosity of their hospitality. I am also indebted to the South African Library and its staff. I cannot imagine a more tranquil and conducive setting than the library's oval Reading Room in which to revise and edit a book. The Managers of the Steele Theological Fund at Cambridge

University awarded me a Studentship towards the cost of my stay. The Master and Fellows of Selwyn College, Cambridge also gave me a grant from the Mitchell Fund towards the cost of my travel. The Principal and Staff of Westcott House, Cambridge, had the courage to allow me to arrange six months of my training for ordination! Without the help of these bodies I would not have been able to come to South Africa at all. Throughout my stay I have been fortunate to make many friends. Imam Rashied Omar has undoubtedly been one of the most charming, thoughtful and prayerful of these. I was deeply touched when, after a meeting one day, he casually remarked that he no longer knew whether he was working for St. George's Cathedral or for the Claremont Mosque. We all took that as a great compliment, Rashied. I feel the same way. I am honoured that you have written the Foreword for this collection of meditations.

I arrived in South Africa with something of a heavy heart, not because I didn't want to be here but because a great friend of mine had died in the most tragic of circumstances shortly before my departure. Fr. Benjamin O'Sullivan O.S.B. was a monk and priest at Ampleforth Abbey in Yorkshire. He and I had been friends since music-making brought us together during student days at Oxford. I have still not had time to adjust to life without his wittiness and kindness or to think through the anguish which led him to take his own life. But my memories of him have kept his presence real for me throughout my six months here. I'm not sure what he would think of such a concept of 'real presence'. He would probably say that it was yet another example of woolly Anglican theology! But I also know that he'd do so with an enormous grin on his face. I am sorry that that smile will not be in England to greet me on my return. He was one of the people who most encouraged me to go to South Africa and I would so much have enjoyed discussing my experiences with him. Alas that is not to be. Nevertheless this is for you Benjamin with my love and thanks. It is also for the many street children with whom I have had contact – especially those of the Yizani Drop-in Centre whose consistent generosity towards me has moved me very deeply. They will probably never know just how much I have received from them. This is also for the staff of the Centre who enable them to achieve such remarkable things. Finally it is for you, Mum and Dad, with my love. Without your love and support none of this great adventure would have been possible. I cannot thank you enough for enabling me to enjoy one of the best six months of my life.

Chris Chivers
Cape Town
November 1996

Introduction to the Second Edition

Echoes of a Rainbow Song was first published in November 1996 under the auspices of St. George's Cathedral Foundation, Cape Town in a limited print-run of 150 copies. At the time it was designed primarily as a 'thank you' for all those with whom I worked in Cape Town and as a collective 'replacement' for the many letters I could – and should – have written to my family and friends in the UK whilst I was away from them.

Since then I have been asked by many of the people who received, bought or borrowed a copy when I was going to make it available to a wider readership. I have hesitated to fulfil their request for a number of reasons. Times change and events move fast – especially in a rapidly-evolving democracy like South Africa – so I have wondered how relevant a second edition would really be. Personal circumstances – not least ordination to the diaconate and the priesthood, marriage and impending fatherhood – have (happily!) given me little time in which to correct, re-edit or re-fashion the book. My mind has been on many other things. And yet nagging away at me has been the conviction that the things of which I wrote actually transcend time or particularity and may thus have a more universal appeal and interest.

Subsequent visits to Cape Town in 1997 (to work on various projects for the Truth and Reconciliation Commission) and in 1998 (on honeymoon), together with my appointment as Canon Precentor of St. George's Cathedral from September 1999, have served to translate intention into action.

The Parish community where I have been so fortunate to serve my curacy has given me a readership for whom to think through the revision.

The invitation in 1998-99 to give talks for the North London Religious Leaders' Forum, The Association of Black Clergy, and Christian Aid, and to preach at Magdalene College, Cambridge and Kent School, Connecticut in the USA, have caused me to return to many of the issues touched on in the book.

So at last, almost three years after I first wrote the bulk of what follows, I am able to publish a second edition, this time primarily as a study resource for my many friends in Friern Barnet – though I hope that it may find a readership further afield as well.

To the first edition I have added some reflections from my journal and from memory. I have also done my best to make corrections where I felt that they were necessary. That I have been able to do so is in no small way due to the proof-reading and grammatical skills of Lynda Capstick, Jane Mason and Sarah Patey. Such errors and imperfections as remain are of course mine and mine alone.

In this whole endeavour I have been grateful for the encouragement, support and interest of family, friends and teachers, too numerous to name, who were kind enough to comment on *Echoes* when it first appeared or from whose wisdom I have greatly benefited over the years. Needless to say they have all influenced my thinking – thus what follows in this book – very greatly.

The publication of a second edition has been made possible through a most generous grant from the Friern Barnet Educational Trust which I gratefully acknowledge.

I also express my thanks to the Rector and Churchwardens of the Parish of Friern Barnet. By making me a generous grant for study-leave, they ensured that the final week re-editing the book was spent in Oxford, amidst the inspiring and imposing surroundings of the Bodleian Library's Radcliffe Camera.

All in all I owe a tremendous amount to a huge number of people. But my greatest debt of thanks is to my wife Mary. It cannot have been easy to live with a husband who simply 'had to disappear' from time to time in order to write new passages or to re-write old ones. Thank you Mary for your forbearance and for urging me to get on with this! It has been wonderful simply to be able to share it all with you. To the dedicatees of the first edition I am delighted and honoured to be able to add your name.

Chris Chivers
Friern Barnet, London
February 1999

1 My soul doth magnify the Lord

Mary has conceived Jesus. She visits Elizabeth. On seeing her aged cousin she breaks into song. And what a song she sings!

On my first Sunday night in Cape Town I find myself in the back row of a set of choir stalls at St. George's Cathedral, doing what I have spent so much of my life doing, singing! The cathedral choir is rehearsing for Evensong and I have joined them. Barry Smith, the choir's Director, stops the singing to make some salient points. We resume our rehearsal of Stanford's *Magnificat in C major.* Glorious unaccompanied singing echoes around the high stone vaulting and I am transported back to Bristol Cathedral where, twenty odd years before, I first experienced this music.

It seems that wherever you go in the Anglican world Stanford in C is to be found. I've heard it in St. Paul's Cathedral, Calcutta in the heat of an Easter Day Evensong when, happily, it was largely drowned out by the overhead fan system! I once wandered into St. Michael's Church in Paris and heard it being rehearsed very ponderously. The Choir of St. Thomas' Church, Fifth Avenue in New York gave a rather over-dramatic interpretation of it when I was there. I've also heard performances in Florence, Italy and even in Sao Paulo,

Brazil! The latter was atrociously unmusical if I recall it correctly.

The Cape Town version is one of the best. It has commitment, drama (but not too much) and fine shaping of the melodic lines. The choir has a gutsy timbre which I like. Be that as it may, there's something just plain comforting about being able to travel the world in the knowledge that Stanford in C will be there to welcome you into the familiar and known quantity which is Anglicanism!

The danger with this is that Mary's song is not much concerned with the familiar and the known. Quite the opposite in fact. She sings about something totally new breaking into the world – she sings about the kingdom of God. This, she tells us, will up-end all known human realities. It will be a kingdom to destroy the principalities and powers of this world as it empowers the poor, the disenfranchised and the powerless.

There's something else which makes me feel a little uneasy about the cosy world of Sir Charles Villiers Stanford and my tendency to fall back on it at every turn in my life. When Mary sings the song she puts her whole being, her soul, behind what she does. When I sing Stanford in C, I certainly put a lot of effort into it. Singing is the most physically demanding of all musical activities. It requires bodily energy. It also requires control in terms of one's breathing and sensitivity to the shape of the musical lines. That necessitates a lot of thought. There's the whole business of the sound production itself – vowels, consonants...the list could go on. So there's lots to do when one sings this Magnificat, and all that occupies most of my mental and emotional space as I perform the piece. Such effort enables me to enjoy the luxuriance of

Stanford's rather grand idiom. I especially savour the expressive tenor phrase at the words 'world without end'. The whole experience moves me. I think that I am close to God. My soul is magnifying the Lord. But am I offering my soul to God or is God just in receipt of my head and body again?

Furthermore, what will be the outcome of my singing? God may or may not have been worshipped. But when I leave the cathedral will I actually go into the world, as the song bids me, ceaselessly to transfigure poverty and deprivation wherever I see it? Or will I just live for the next performance of Stanford in C, wherever that may be?

The Sunday morning after Archbishop Njongonkulu's Enthronement he celebrates the Eucharist at St. Mary's Church, Guguletu which is in the township where he grew up. Well, to be accurate the Eucharist takes place in a very large and splendid yellow-and-white striped marquee closeby the church. Choirs drawn from four townships – Langa, Nyanga, Guguletu and Khayelitsha – combine to sing the evocative *African Marimba Mass* and some tremendously vibrant Freedom songs. I find it all immensely moving and I feel that I am close to God. Certainly I am close to tears.

Afterwards I try to communicate my thanks to Mlamli Mfenyana who is the Vicar of Holy Cross, Nyanga and Musical Director for the Service.

'I came all the way to South Africa to hear that sound, Father. Thank you so much.'

I think that he is also overcome by how much it has meant to me. But conversation with this animated priest is swiftly brought to a conclusion by the choirs who, in post-service exhuberance, strike up with some of the songs we heard a little earlier, this time with an ad-hoc marimba accompaniment. Young people gyrate and clap to the pulsating rhythms. This soon catches on amongst those of us who are left inside the marquee. Even my typical British reserve gives way a little as my hips tentatively begin to wind themselves into action! The singing moves me even more now than it had in the service because it is so spontaneous. A weekend of celebrations, which began in the Enthronement liturgy with the planned splendour of Parry's *I was glad,* is culminating in what Christian Hartnick calls 'holy chaos!'

As I stand in the marquee I reflect that there is a powerful little parable in the weekend's musical journey, especially for the churches I have known back home in England. Mary gave her whole soul to God in song. She sang to a God who had made chaos out of her young life by the intrusion upon it of a pregnancy which wasn't planned and which must have been both a disruption and an embarrassment for her. Hers was a life which had suddenly been caught up in the realm of the holy and this inevitably meant a fair amount of chaos for her. If only the Church of England could get the balance right between the two. It's often either all holiness – all pomp and splendour – which alienates some people, or it's all chaos – all 'do it yourself hand-waving hymn sandwiches' – which alienates others.

The Church of the Province of Southern Africa is far from perfect. It's part of the Christian Church after all! Churches need the message of redemption as much as, if not more so than, anyone else. But the CPSA does seem to be quite at ease with 'holy chaos'. This I suspect means that it can give body, head and soul to God in song more than the folks back home can, more indeed than I seem able to do. This is so because in its worship it represents the whole of human life to God - our carefully planned hopes and the utterly unexpected situations in which we find ourselves. For if we're brutally honest, our lives are a bizarre mixture of the holy and the chaotic. Aren't they?

2 And my spirit hath rejoiced in God my Saviour

Physically speaking my stay in Cape Town is dominated by two factors – the weather and Table Mountain. The climate in the Cape is extremely changeable. You can literally experience four seasons in a day if not in an hour! Table Mountain is of course utterly changeless. Almost all directions are given by reference to this immovable stone structure. After a while one tends to take its presence for granted but its towering grandeur cannot be ignored for long.

If the sky is clear and the sun is out its rays produce a dazzling interplay of light and shadow on the mountain's craggy exterior. This creates a pewter-like colour I have seen nowhere else in the world. But if the famous 'table-cloth' of cloud has rolled down from the mountain top and is covering the rock face the whole of the City Bowl is bleak and dark.

Wherever I have stayed in the city I have enjoyed close proximity to the mountain. In Oranjezicht just up from the City Bowl, at Barry Smith's house and at the Deanery, the cable-car was very close. At Michael Keall's flat in Rondebosch my bedroom window faced the University of Cape Town and the mountain behind it. In the Bokaap, the city's famous 'Malay Quarter', I could look past the minaret of one of the area's many mosques to enjoy another angle onto the cable-car side of the mountain.

I have often lived in places of great physical beauty but nothing compares with Cape Town! Waking up to a mountain has been a thrilling and fascinating experience for me. When the sun has been shining Table Mountain has immediately lifted my spirits. I have felt that inner excitement which must have been Elizabeth's when she saw her cousin Mary and the babe in her womb leapt for joy. I have wanted to leap out of bed and throw myself into the tasks ahead of me. But when the clouds have descended and I've hardly been able to see the mountain, I've just rolled over in bed and dived underneath the duvet!

Odd, isn't it, that my commitment and enthusiasm for life each day is so dependent on the weather! I wonder if my faith is as fickle?

One grey morning in October I walk somewhat dejectedly down Wale Street from my home in the Bokaap. I pass the cathedral, looking beyond it to the mountain which is covered in cloud, and turn into Adderley Street to head for the Cathedral Foundation's offices. I am dejected and heavy-footed this morning because, with only two days to go before we launch a huge project for one hundred and twenty-eight children to explore the work of the Truth and Reconciliation Commission, we are still far from having things sewn up. Each day seems to bring with it new – and bigger – problems! Yesterday I was working on our latest logistical nightmare – how to transport the children in from communities scattered all across the Western Cape. What on earth will today bring I wonder?

8

I reach the entrance to Regis House and stop to pick up some messages from the security staff. Then I head off to the lift. From behind me I hear someone shouting 'Baas, baas!' I turn around and I find myself confronted by Sammy, who sells fruit on the pavement in front of the building, animatedly waving an orange at me!

'Baas, baas...I have the oranges for you.'

'The oranges, Sammy?'

'Yes, baas...you remember the oranges you ask me for.'

'Oranges, Sammy?'

I look blankly at him.

'Yes baas...oranges for the children.'

I continue to look blankly at him.

'You not like these oranges, baas?' he asks me, obviously confused by my failure to remember why we should be discussing oranges at all.

'Goodness, Sammy. I'm so sorry...'

At last I have remembered that I ordered oranges for us to use at the climax of the project in an adaptation of the Western Christingle.

So I repeat my apology for failing to respond to him. But all too late I fear. For Sammy now looks dejected and a bit cross.

'You ask me for oranges...you not want them?'

'No, of course I want them Sammy. I'm sorry. My mind was miles away. I'd forgotten all about the oranges. I'm so sorry.'

'That's okay, baas,' Sammy replies in a more generous way than I deserve from him.

'How much do they cost?'

Sammy smiles broadly.

'You have them baas... no charge... it's for the children...'

I thank him profusely. But I realise only too painfully, as I do so, that there has in fact been great cost in this transaction – the literal cost to Sammy of a whole box of oranges (an immense sacrifice for any street-trader to make) but also the inner cost he has paid through my terrible inattentiveness to him. For despite Sammy's smile I can sense that I have hurt his feelings.

My unnecessary self-preoccupation has prevented me from having my spirits lifted by Sammy's enthusiastic generosity. And in the process I have taken the edge right off a moment to which, I suspect, he had been looking forward for days.

3 For he hath regarded

In the run-up to Archbishop Njongonkulu's Enthronement I receive a fax from Mary Rogers, an English woman who has lived in South Africa for many years. It details the points from which the Communion will be distributed to the two-thousand-strong congregation. The letter opens 'Dear Chris...' and then continues 'Herewith, as promised, the details...Regards, Mary.'

As I wrest the fax from the machine I wonder, as I often do, what is meant by 'Regards, so-and-so.' Does it mean that Mary holds me in regard? That is a flattering thought! Is it just a social convention? Or does it mean that somehow she is actually picturing me, literally 'regarding me', as she writes and dispatches her message? This is a comforting thought as communication by fax is so terribly impersonal.

Regards. One short word.

Can it really overcome the distance between my fax machine and hers? Does it actually link Mary and me together in some kind of relationship?

I am travelling into Cape Town one beautiful August morning on the Metro when I begin to feel very uneasy indeed. All my fellow passengers seem to be staring at me. At least that's what I think.

Sensing that I am regarded with suspicion I avoid eye contact. Why is my presence so strange to them I wonder?

I have down-dressed since my arrival in the Cape, avoiding my usual smart shirt, tie and jacket so as not to seem too prosperous and business-like! I know that I don't look touristy. Furthermore I've tried to blend in with the more informal character of local fashions and though I've never been especially noted for my fashion-consciousness I haven't, I think, done a bad job!

Are they looking at me, or am I looking uncomfortably at myself through their eyes? Is it that I'm bouncing off them, back onto myself, my most deep-seated fears as to the kind of person I really am? Another bit of Chris Chivers' paranoia perhaps?

I decide that it is too early in the morning for such heavy probings of my psyche. I bury my head in a copy of *The Cape Times*. It is large enough to hide behind. It is a convenient barrier between myself and anyone else.

'I don't care what they think,' I say to myself. But on the inside of course I care very much. It matters crucially how I'm regarded – even by strangers – whatever temporary barriers I erect to shut them out.

I scamper down the steps of St. George's Cathedral as I make for Adderley Street on my way to the Metro Station. I must get the 5.30 p.m. train to Rondebosch. I have only an hour in which to travel home, shower, change and be ready for a supper engagement. It is now 5.22 p.m. I break into a sort of run!

'Baas, baas...' A young voice, which echoes in the Cathedral's North Porch, stops me in my tracks.

I swerve round to see Johann who is fourteen years old or thereabouts. Johann is one of Cape Town's many street children. He is a regular at the Yizani Drop-in Centre. No doubt he has just woken up from his afternoon nap in the porch where he sometimes sleeps.

'Father (he addresses me more personally now)...please Father, I need forty cents for a phone call.'

'Who on earth is he going to phone ?' I think to myself.

He must be lying. He must want the money for thinners or glue. So I open my hands to indicate that I have no money. This is also a lie.

'But Father, please Father.'

'Johann I don't have any money.'

I emphasise what I say with more hand gesticulation. He changes tack. I look at my watch. It is now 5.26. I'm going to miss that blessed train.

'Father you must come and see us at the Centre.'

'I will be coming on Friday Johann,' Friday being the day on which I normally spend the morning at the Yizani Drop-in Centre.

'Promise Father?'

'Yes of course Johann.'

At least I'm telling the truth about something now though I must sound a little impatient to him.

'That's good Father', he says as he smiles, retreats to his blanket and probably to his bag of glue. I seize my chance.

'I must go now Johann...see you on Friday.'

At last I am free to scamper down Adderley Street. I've missed the 5.30 p.m. train. But there's one at 5.37 p.m..

Supper that night is wonderful - roast chicken with all the usual trimmings and Cape Brandy Tart to follow.

13

The following Friday I walk up the hill to Bree Street where the Yizani Drop-in Centre is situated.

'Hi Father!'

Johann greets me with a big smile and a cheerful wave. Then he returns to the picture he's drawing.

Ten minutes later he brings it to show me.

'It's for you Father.'

He has drawn himself and some of his friends. He has signed the picture with his name and one word which he's mis-spelt in Afrikaans: 'lefd' (it should be 'liefde'). It means 'love'.

I am delighted to receive his picture. It represents another break-through in our relationship. But I am swiftly overcome by feelings of guilt and anxiety. I don't really deserve his love. After all I didn't pay him much attention the other day when I was rushing for the train. I didn't give him the forty cents he wanted. That at least was probably wise. But less forgivable is the fact that I regarded him as just an inconvenience preventing me from making my supper engagement. Yet he nevertheless regards me with affection.

That's difficult too because I'm only going to be here for six months and I don't want him to become too attached to me.

'Don't do it to yourself, Johann. Please don't,' I say to myself. 'Don't put your faith in me. Don't start regarding me as the one who'll be here to sort things out for you because I won't be.'

Another voice sounds within me.

'You're erecting those barriers again Chris. Why have you come to Cape Town in the first place if all you're going to do is to cocoon yourself from people? You don't want

Johann to regard you as someone he can depend on, when he needs you, yet it does matter to you that he regards you with respect. It matters too what all those passengers on the train think about you and what Mary thinks. You can't have it both ways.'

I send the contents of this meditation, pretty much as they appear here, to three friends – to Matt, who like me is an ordinand but on placement in Chicago; to Paul, another ordinand who is still in Cambridge; and to Seth, who left Westcott in the summer when he was ordained Deacon to serve in the parish church at Golders Green in London. I need them to hear what I'm feeling. They're good at dealing with my mixed-up emotions. I miss their company and all their insights.

I close the letters, which accompany copies of the meditation, not with 'Regards, Chris', but with real affection – 'love, Chris'. I place them on the pile for posting.

'Regards, Chris', 'love, Chris', what's the difference? Either way I am expressing my dependence on Matt, Paul and Seth and on their judgement and affection. If these single words can, as I believe they do, overcome the thousands of miles between Cape Town, Chicago, Cambridge and London they must surely be able to bridge the shorter gaps between myself and Johann, the passengers who sit opposite me on the Metro and Mary whose fax machine is just the other side of town.

Absence makes the heart grow fonder, so the saying goes. If only closeness could make my heart more openly loving to those who stare me in the face.

4 The lowliness of his handmaiden

The Arch, which is situated in the Hall next to St. George's Cathedral, dispenses bread and soup to the homeless or to township dwellers who have come into the city in search of work. It is full of characters! One-armed John pitches up most mornings. Life cannot be at all easy for him on the streets but he is always cheerful and full of conversation. We often talk about American films for which he has a great passion! He won't however accept any help when it comes to him carrying his soup and bread to one of the tables in order to eat it. He prefers to make several trips, displaying an independence of mind which has doubtless developed through years of toughing it out on the streets.

One morning John is followed in the queue by a woman who hands Eddie Shepherd, the manager, a note. He and I then read it. 'Please Sir. No money today for soup and bread. Will bring money tomorrow. Promise.' Sadly I do not know this woman's name. She is deaf and dumb. But without hesitation we both sort out some bread and soup for her. We also tell her that she needn't bring the money next time. The odd thirty cents is really neither here nor there. We are so touched by her note that we'd gladly give her cups of soup and bread for the rest of the morning .

As I look across the counter at this gracious woman I wonder whether she has shown me what real lowliness is?

The concept of lowliness has troubled me for a long time. The Church teaches its importance. It celebrates Mary's role as the woman who joyfully accepted the task of bringing the Christ-child into the world. But I find the narrative which has been woven around the great mystery of the Incarnation terribly unconvincing. Would Mary really have rejoiced in an unexpected pregnancy? Isn't it more likely that she'd have been terrified at the prospect of life as a single mother and consequently life as an outcast in society? I strongly suspect that the facts have been shrouded in a lot of pious nonsense written mostly by men whose chief interest is the subservience of women. To them lowliness meant obedience and it was in their interests that women should exhibit such obedience. It greatly troubles me that this should be the case – that the gospels should set up a dynamic of expectancy in which this kind of lowliness is a chief requirement. For it seems to me that what is being said is that women in particular must just accept whatever is dished out to them. For in this song God 'regards' Mary, God favours her, because she possesses this quality of 'lowliness'. She accepts whatever comes her way without questioning it. I find that profoundly disturbing. Perhaps I am reading too much into the original narrative. Perhaps the song and the gospel stories which support it are trying to emphasise something I can go along with. Perhaps they are really saying that all of us must, like Mary, accept the talents and responsibilities God calls us to use and to fulfil. Which is fine. But that's not the way the text has been used in the hands of a largely male-dominated Church structure.

There is a fine line between cheerful obedience to God's call and choiceless subservience to a male-dominated mind-set. One of my favourite hymns – *Come down, O Love divine* – talks about 'true lowliness of heart, which takes the humbler part.' That's fair enough too. Humble service is one thing. You can choose to serve. But passive acceptance of oppression is something different. You have no choice but to endure it.

I look again at the woman across the counter. She hasn't of course shown lowliness at all. To see it that way is to imagine that she actually chose to beg for what should be hers and everyone else's by right – some daily bread. But her 'choice', such as it is, has not been made freely. She begs because she is poor – because she is a victim of a society which allows her to be so. And though we've fed her I'm left wondering whether we haven't ourselves just passively accepted an unjust system. We have done what the world isn't doing. Thank God in one sense that this is the case. But the song Mary sings is about overturning the injustices of the world, not simply about patching them up. Surely our goal must be the eradication of the injustice of her poverty – indeed the creation of a world in which every person can choose to be lowly and not simply be forced to accept the lowliness which is thrust upon them.

5 For behold from henceforth

St. Paul said some things in his letters which seem pretty unpalatable these days. But his writings nevertheless contain many passages which have a timeless quality about them. Of these one of my favourites is about 'time' itself – 'Now is the time to wake out of sleep for now is our salvation nearer than when we first believed'. From henceforth. From now onwards.

To say that my six months in Cape Town are hectic would be somewhat of an understatement! I'm literally run off my feet with one project after the next. This suits me down to the ground. Arguably I enjoy the best six months of my life. But being busy I find that my time is marked by a succession of delaying tactics!

'I'm tied up just now. I'll be with you in a few moments.'

There are other variations:

'I'm in a meeting just now. I'll ring you this afternoon.'

'Would you mind just holding for a moment? I've a call on the other line.'

Most lives these days are punctuated by similar such phrases. This is one of the perils of life in a world-wide communication network. But it is sad that we expend so much energy avoiding real communication simply because we're trying to communicate with too many people! This is because we have become helplessly enmeshed in a world which judges worth by the level of activity it perceives. If you're not seen to be at full stretch you're lazy. We have lost the balance between 'doing' and 'being'. Our philosophy is 'it's all or nothing, now'. But that's a hopelessly short-term view of things.

When St. Paul spoke of the need to 'wake out of sleep', I don't think he especially had the indolent in mind. Most of the communities he dealt with were in fact so busy having religious 'experiences', that he literally struggled to keep their feet on the ground! Paul did not want people to think that being a Christian meant one had endlessly to be doing God's work. He wanted his communities simply to wake up to the reality of God's kingdom - to the now of God's presence. Doing would of course have to follow. But if I think that I am bringing in the kingdom more speedily by all the rushing around that I do I am much mistaken. I shall be a more effective citizen of the kingdom if I take time off from doing just to be myself.

A phone call containing some bad news is just one issue too many for me to cope with one day in the Foundation offices. I have to escape. I take a bus to Sea Point and I walk along the beach. I run through all the things which are on my mind. I pick up pebbles and throw them into the sea. This is a kind of therapy for me. I throw them away and let go of all the things on my mind. I do so because I know that all those pebbles will one day return to the beach just as all those issues will come back into my life. But for now I must let go of them. I must create some space in which to be before I return to all the things which I must do. I promise myself that from now onwards I will make this a weekly routine. But I've said that before.

6 All generations shall call me blessed

One Friday in early October I arrive at the Yizani Drop-in Centre to find it fairly empty. Normally there are between twenty-five and thirty street children present but this morning there are just a handful. Some of the regulars however greet me. Ivan, Daniel, Patrick, Andrew and the two Michaels are busy playing dominoes or kerem – which is a game like pool played with cue sticks on a board with four 'pockets' and using two sets of differently-coloured counters.

At 9.30 a.m. Johann saunters in. He is invariably late and tired-looking hence his nick-name the 'sleeping beauty'. He has a bad gash on his right hand which I dress for him. Then he joins the domino-playing group. I play kerem with Andrew and, greatly to my surprise and his, I beat him. This means that I must stay on to meet the next challenger.

Right on cue Marvin arrives. He is around fifteen years old, originally from East Ridge on Mitchell's Plain and is highly articulate and charming. He wipes the floor with me on the kerem table in about five minutes flat. He offers me a two hundred rand note as a consolation prize. Heaven alone knows how he came by it. I dread to think. But I take custody of it for a few moments much to his consternation! Having returned the note to him we sit down next to one another.

Marvin greatly enjoys drawing, writing and reading aloud. He is good at all three. This morning he begins to draw by taking out some small change and tracing the surface of the coins to produce an impression of them. Having traced the coins he labels them. At the bottom of the page he writes a caption.

'From mouny you can get food. You can drive your own car'.

He follows this up with another line.

'You no what if I have mouny I by lucksery'.

What follows between us has established itself into a regular pattern over the weeks. We chat about the pictures and what he has said. I ask him which 'lucksery' he has in mind. Without a pause for thought he says 'chocolate'. Then he begins work on another drawing. Like the previous one whose theme was money – an obvious one for a street child – this drawing picks up on another recurring theme – foreigners and their countries of origin. There is of course an escapism about such subject-matter for a street child. Money and foreign countries represent 'dream' worlds which are tantalisingly near and yet frustratingly far from their grasp. They live in Cape Town surrounded by the business community. They live in the areas most visited by tourists. So near and yet so far.

Marvin has drawn a 'China-man'. He labels the drawing. He asks me about my own country and I draw it for him very roughly. What happens next is also part of our routine. He asks more personal questions and he does so by writing them down. He wants to know something about my parents.

'What', he writes, 'mouther and fauther doe?'

I scribble a reply.

He stops to think carefully about what to write next. This is his characteristic approach to such written conversations which he fills with long pauses for thought.

After a while he writes down three 'thoughts'.

'Love is a pian that no docter can explian'.

'I love all but I trus no one'.

'I broke my mouthers hart to srole in Cape Town. Sorry Mumm'.

Marvin's interest in my parents has obviously sparked off this train of reflections for him. Up until now I have been both immersed 'in' the conversation with Marvin and also in a sense 'outside' of it observing his thought-patterns in an effort to understand the way he thinks and to assess what his needs might be. But as he makes himself increasingly vulnerable to me, in the thoughts he writes, so he touches all my own vulnerabilities.

The third in the series of his 'thoughts' has set off a particularly strong set of emotional responses inside of me. Pity, compassion and a great sense of sorrow combine to bring tears to my eyes. We look at each other and share a similar sense of pain for Marvin is also close to tears. He points to my piece of paper. I must now write something. But what? I will have to trust my instincts. Any objectivity I had has all but disappeared. I scribble a line and hand it to him.

'I'm sure your Mum knows that you love her.'

Marvin holds the paper and reads it very slowly. He pauses to think about what I have written and his face begins to break into the kind of smile we all produce through tears. He smiles through the pain. Perhaps his tremendous burden of guilt has been lifted a little.

Marvin left home because he had to. The abuse he was suffering at the hands of his father forced him out. But he left knowing how painful his departure was for his mother.

How utterly tragic to find oneself in a situation like Marvin's. As he continues to draw I gaze through the window of the Centre which faces Table Mountain.

I will lift up mine eyes unto the hills from whence cometh my help.

Contrasting images flit through my mind. I picture my own mother. I, like Marvin, have a sense of the pain which she feels at my being away. I hear it in her choked voice as each precious telephone conversation draws to a close. Marvin has heightened my awareness of this. He has also made me more aware of how blessed I am in having a mother like mine and in not having a family situation like his. Marvin's mother means all the world to him. That is why he feels so guilty. My mother means the same to me. I identify with his feelings of guilt because I too am away from home. But I can go back. Marvin can't.

Mary the mother of Jesus. Mary blessed through all the generations. I wonder what she felt when her son went 'strolling' off into Galilee one day never to return? I wonder too what he felt about leaving her behind?

7 For he that is mighty hath magnified me

Ivan is without doubt one of the cheekiest, most entertaining and outwardly happy of the Yizani street children. He's in his mid-teens. I'd say that he was about fifteen. Most Fridays he challenges me to a game of kerem. During our early bouts I was hopelessly outclassed. I played the game like pool or snooker. I concentrated too much on angles and not enough on adventure! I really wasn't much competition for Ivan. But as the weeks have gone on so he has sensed that I'm improving and becoming a much more worthy challenger. And he's been immensely generous about all this. Indeed he's been a model teacher showing me where and how I must strike the counter to achieve better results.

'You spiel good now, Chris,' he says one Friday in mid-October. I have given my best showing to date.

The following Friday I actually take a game off him. I do so because I have accumulated enough skill to be more adventurous. So I take some chances and win.

Ivan smiles and congratulates me. 'We'll spiel again next week, Chris...'

These days people are not much attracted to a concept of God as the Mighty One. I suppose that it has too much of a militaristic ring about it. But the term 'mighty' does not have to suggest a God of power and domination.

We are after all still happy to sing about a God who is our 'refuge and strength'. To say that God is mighty is really to say the same thing. So we need to see the word as describing a God who sustains us, who is what Table Mountain is to Cape Town, a crag and stronghold.

To talk then of a mighty God is to talk of a being whose stability allows us the flexibility to become fully what we are.

I always remember my father talking about the tennis matches he played against Jo Durie when she was a teenager and long before she had reached the top ten in Women's Tennis. He described the way in which she played him until the moment she could beat him. Then he said that she stopped challenging him and moved onto someone else.

I have often wondered how Dad felt about that. Knowing how much he loved coaching and how good he was at it I suspect that he was simply delighted that she was progressing so well and so fast. But Dad is also a great competitor. I don't remember receiving too many 'gift' points from him when we played tennis together! Indeed I never actually beat him in all the years we played. So I suspect that a small part of him was more than a little irked when Jo beat him.

Skill and knowledge represent power. Being a great teacher my father never abused the power which was at the end of his racquet. As a coach he had a wealth of tactical knowledge, great ball sense and terrific racquet control. He could place the ball anywhere he wanted it to go! He could have kept back some of that knowledge to ensure that he was always on top. That's what bad teachers do – who only teach to boost their own egos. They give so much but they never give the game away entirely. When I played my father we fought tooth and nail until the final point. I didn't ever beat him. But this wasn't because he hadn't taught me some vital aspect of the game which would have enabled me to take the final step to victory. It was because I simply wasn't good enough! He gave me all the tools and skills. He equipped me, encouraged me and gave me tactical methods to hang the whole game on. He empowered all his pupils in a similar way. I just wasn't one of the better ones! In doing so he taught me what true education is all about.

When we've played kerem Ivan has had every reason to keep all his skill and knowledge of the game to himself. Street children don't after all find themselves in many situations where they are in control, where they have the power and hold all the trump cards. But Ivan hasn't held back at all. He's taught me, encouraged me and in the end given me the tools with which to beat him. I find it remarkable that he hasn't abused what little hold he potentially had over me. It is a great tribute to a great guy. But it is also a testimony to the graciousness and generosity of the human spirit in adversity.

Ivan has shown me what true mightiness is as my father did before him. It means empowering and liberating others. Would that the mighty of this world could do the same for him.

8 And holy is his Name

South Africa celebrates its National Heritage Day on September 24th with a public holiday. President Mandela helps the nation to hallow the name of Erich Sontango, composer of *Nkosi sikelel i'Afrika,* by declaring his grave a national monument. I meanwhile join thousands of others in Cape Town's Company Gardens. The weather is depressingly cold and wet for mid-September. Nothing however is going to dampen the spirits of those who have come to revel in a day of street-theatre, jazz, funk, soul, big-band and marimba music.

A familiar group of street children bound up to me, swinging away to the off-beat rhythms of the rap-artist who is on stage at that moment.

'Hello, Chrees!' The crispness of the English 'Chris' does not translate well into their Afrikaans. But three months into my stay in the Cape they have all learnt a version of my name.

'Hi, guys,' I reply, using a collective noun not normally part of my vocabulary but which is definitely part of the local lingo. Using it makes it easier to relate to them and it gets me round the fact that I can't seem to remember all their names.

'How are you, guys?' I enquire.

'Hungry, Chrees,' they reply with a directness I have come to expect from them. 'Can you buy us some food please Chrees?'

The more they use my name the more guilty I feel at not knowing theirs. I could ask them of course. But I've done that so many times before that they must be fed up with my inability to remember even their names.

'Chrees, Chrees, Chrees...' they implore.

My name is their route to one of the day's goals – food.

And holy is his Name.

Doubtless the day will hold other goals for them. For sure they will spend some of it attempting to pick the pockets of nameless souls for valuables and trinkets. And they'll also beg for food from people whose names they don't know. A gathering of thousands represents a golden opportunity for them! But they won't steal from me. Of that I am sure. Instead, because they know my name, they will use it to prize open the door of my conscience until I feed them. And so they should! If I'm gratified that they know my name (which I am) – even though I'm too lazy to learn theirs – I must expect them to rip the door to my conscience right off its hinges. For we're not only to be known by our names. By our deeds should others know that our names really mean something – that they are holy.

I go off in search of food for the children though I don't tell them that. It'll be a nice surprise for them. By the time I get back with some food they have disappeared.

Nice though the music is I am getting a little fed up with the steady drizzle which is falling on me. So I take a wander down Government Avenue towards the Cathedral. There on the North Porch I encounter another group of street children – two Yizani boys surrounded by a group of girls.

'Hi, Chrees,' the boys shout as they wave enthusiastically at me.

'Hi, guys,' is again my reply. And as I walk up the steps to the North Porch that greeting does, in this most politically correct of countries, for girls too! The two boys both know, like the previous ones, that using my name means a potential meal. In this situation, because they know me, it also means that they can act as a bridge between me and the whole needy little group which sits at the top of the steps. If they can pull it off, and I indeed produce some food for them, it'll do their standing with the girls no end of good.

After my abortive attempt to feed the last Yizani group I had decided that if I met any more street children I knew, asking for food, I would ask them to wait whilst I went off to get some. It is after all a public holiday – surely a day for handing out 'treats'? So the boys on the North Porch don't have to work too hard to persuade me to buy them some food. But the situation has a slightly different dynamic to it this time because I know their names. I am speaking to Patrick, a tall and immensely polite fifteen-year-old and to Daniel, a smaller, somewhat toothless and extrovert thirteen-year-old. It satisfies me greatly that I can personalise this encounter at least by using their names. I rush off to buy some hot samosas and some biscuits.

I offer Patrick and Daniel the goodies for the whole group and they thank me profusely. But they do not use my name. Instead they call me 'Sir'.

'Thank you, Sir...Kind Sir...Very kind Sir'.

I understand their subservience. Years of oppression has taught so many people a model of relationship which is based on 'Yes Sir, No Sir, Three Bags full Sir'. Patrick and Daniel have momentarily broken out of that. But as soon as I have put myself in the helping role they retreat to the use of a familiar stereotype. And holy is his name.

Despite my frustration at this, part of me remains pleased that I have been able to feed them. I have a genuine instinct, like most human beings, to help others less fortunate than myself. But why is it so important for me that they see my name as holy, that it is Chrees feeding them and not anyone else? What, after all, is in a name?

9 And his mercy is on them that fear him

Drawing out cash these days is as straightforward a business for me in Cape Town as it is anywhere else in the world. I just use my visa card at any one of the banks on or just off Adderley Street. My request is beamed back by satellite to my Lloyd's Bank branch in the U.K. It takes a little longer to obtain authorisation than it does when I'm at home but the delay is only a matter of a few seconds.

During the lunch-hour I often nip out to use the Standard Bank cash machine which is near the St. George's Cathedral Foundation offices in Adderley Street. The Bank is in St. George's Mall – a pedestrianised street parallel to Adderley – and the cash machines are conveniently located to the right of the main entrance.

One Monday in September I nip into Mark's (a sandwich bar) and then on to the Bank. I step off the Mall and am very pleased to see that the lunchtime queues have died down. Fifty Rand is all that I need to keep me going for the next few days. I push my card into the vacant machine. As I do so I hear a little voice crying out 'Chrees, Chrees'.

The screen in front of me reads: 'Do not be distracted during your transaction'. Some hope! I turn around, cancelling my request as I do so, to see 'Snaff' who is about eight years old. He is lying behind the glass doors of the bank's main entrance. He seems barely able to raise his head off the floor. Nevertheless he is determined to attract my attention. I go over to see what's the matter with him. As I move closer I can see that his face is covered with very purple bruises.

'What on earth has happened to you?' I ask anxiously.

'Boy...boy...hit...me,' comes his stammered reply as he tries unsuccessfully to hold back his tears.

The look of fear on his face is very distressing.

'Who hit you,' I ask.

'Older boy,' he replies.

I gently persist.

'Which older boy, Snaff?'

'Older boy, Chrees.'

I realise that he is of course too frightened to tell me which boy. It was in fact a bit stupid of me to ask him to do so. So I don't bother to question him further as to why his face looks in such a terrible mess, because I know that he's just too upset and frightened to tell me. I sit beside him and hold his hand instead.

'Snaff' is not my young friend's real name. It is a nick-name which originated in the fact that we have played a lot of the card game 'snap' together at the Yizani Drop-in Centre. Snaff cannot say 'snap'. It always comes out as 'snaff'. Hence the nick-name which he likes very much.

As I hold his hand, questions as to what has happened to him and why persist. Of late I have not seen much of Snaff at the Centre. I wonder whether one of the older Yizani boys has roughed him up a few times and made him afraid to come? I'll probably never know the answer to that. What's important right now is that I try to patch Snaff up as best I can.

'Do you want something to eat Snaff?' I ask.

'Yes please Chrees. I'm very hungry.'

'Okay, Snaff, what would you like? A sandwich?'

'Yes please.'

The mention of food has already lifted his spirits a little. He begins to smile.

'Cheese? Ham? What kind of sandwich would you like?'

From a more smiling countenance comes a swift reply. 'Cheese please, Chrees.'

So I ask Snaff to wait for me in the bank foyer whilst I potter off to Mark's again to purchase the sandwich.

When I return I find Snaff being bawled out of the foyer by a young bank teller. My hackles rise and immediately I vent my anger.

'What on earth are you doing?' I shout at the clerk.

'Shifting this skelm out of the bank,' he replies.

His use of the word 'skelm', which means 'rogue' in Afrikaans, really riles me.

'He isn't a skelm...and...and can't you see that he's been beaten up and is frightened out of his skin?'

I can barely contain my anger.

'That's not my problem,' the young teller calmly and dismissively replies.

I realise that this is a verbal battle which is not worth fighting. Reason is simply not going to conquer this kind of ignorance and prejudice. So I turn around and concentrate on Snaff who understandably looks timid and shell-shocked.

'Come on,' I say to him, 'let's go and have some lunch.'

I put my arm around him and, watched by the small crowd which has gathered during the confrontation, I escort Snaff to the steps of the Cathedral nearby. 'Shame man...poor little boy,' I hear one passer-by remark.

Shame indeed.

We sit on the steps and I give him the sandwich he asked for, together with a can of Coke and a Kit-Kat. He receives them with much gratitude and is soon tucking into the sandwich. But noticing that I haven't any lunch myself he offers me a finger of the Kit-Kat. It is a touching gesture on his part.

We don't talk at first because we are both too busy eating. But nevertheless I experience a real sense of communion between the two of us. Just what the Eucharist should be, I think to myself. Fear is being conquered by mutual love – if that's not too grand an analogy to draw. But as we finish eating my anger, which has temporarily been stemmed by our koinonia, returns with avengeance. I'm angry at the bank teller's appalling insensitivity but I'm also angry because I feel so helpless. I have fed Snaff and patched him up a bit. Certainly he seems a little more cheerful now. I've done what I hope any reasonable human being would do. I've shown him a bit of 'mercy'. But there's not much else that I can do for him.

I can't, for example, make him come to the Centre. That would probably be counter-productive anyway given the circumstances which I suspect led up to my finding Snaff hiding in the bank. All I can do now is to return him to the streets from which he came – a little more cheerful perhaps on the surface but no doubt as fearful underneath as he was an hour ago. I hope that there'll be others who will have mercy on him. But of that, of course, there can be no guarantee.

10 Throughout all generations

About two thirds of the way through my time at St. George's, Chris Ahrends, the Sub Dean, spots me at my desk looking tired and worn-out. He doesn't have to say anything. I know what his diagnosis will be. We have spoken about it before. I am suffering from 'compassion fatigue'. There's only so much any human being can take in terms of the demands placed upon them by the needy. But I find that hard to come to terms with. God's mercy endures throughout the generations. Mine doesn't even seem able to last out six months.

During the 1960s and 70s the people who lived in Cape Town's District Six were forcibly removed from their homes to new township communities organised along strictly racial lines. One of the most diverse and colourful communities in the world was systematically destroyed in a matter of years.

In mid-October I visit the District Six Museum with Vivien Harber and Rashied Omar. We are in search of photographic images of the apartheid years for our children's workshop on truth and reconciliation.

A member of the Cathedral's congregation, who works in the museum, fields our enquiries. We have already selected negative images of the apartheid years, like the famous photograph of Hector Petersen's body being carried by another child during the Soweto riots. What we need to complement these are some positive images of life under apartheid which will show the resilience of the human spirit amidst terrible oppression.

We look at a very striking picture of children playing cricket in the last street of homes left standing in the district. Then our guide points across the room to an elderly man. It was this man, she informs us, who gave the museum all the street signs which are such a powerful and painful reminder of a lost community. He had kept them hidden for years in his house. He was supposed to have consigned them, together with all the rubble from the demolished houses of the district, to the bottom of Table Bay in order to help extend the foreshore. It was this man to whom the government of the time had given the responsibility for the breaking-up of the district.

We are stunned to be in the presence of someone who represents all that was most evil about apartheid. For this man implemented a callous plan of action, the consequences of which will reverberate through the Western Cape for generations. Yet here he is assisting a project which memorialises all the suffering he had such a hand in causing.

I cannot reconcile the two things. I'm loath to reach up to the shelf of platitudes which is always close at hand for religious people and to start talking too freely about sin, repentance and forgiveness. My mind simply cannot encapsulate what he did to District Six and what he's doing now.

Then again neither can I give an account of the fact that human beings from across the generations have shown themselves to be capable of appalling evil and of great kindness and thoughtfulness often at one and the same time. I know that it just won't do to say that their evil traits can be explained away by madness or that in their good actions the hand of God was reasserting itself. That's terribly bad theology which dodges the issue altogether. But that's as far as I can go. I simply cannot penetrate further the mystery of evil. No doubt that has been the case for my fellow human beings throughout the generations. But my mind cannot stop wrestling with the problem nonetheless.

On 31 October we launch the Children's Ubuntu Project at the cathedral. Children come from all over the Western Cape for a day workshop to explore South Africa's history - past, present and future. We begin in song and we end with a candle-lighting ceremony which bridges every divide of culture, creed or generation. It is a day of hopes and dreams. But it is also a day when we confront painful realities.

An hour into the day I find myself sitting amongst an animated group of nine- and ten-year-olds. They are discussing a photograph taken – they do not know this – in Guguletu during the 1976 uprisings. On the left of the picture a small black boy attempts to scamper away from a soldier – brandishing a huge truncheon – and two other soldiers close by, one of whom has a sickening grin on his face.

The children begin by considering the boy himself. What has he done, they wonder, to provoke these men into pursuing him? Perhaps he has stolen something? Perhaps he has vandalised the house from which he seems to be fleeing?

'But why,' someone asks, 'is a policeman about to hit him for this...hitting is wrong.'

'If an adult hits a child it's child abuse,' says one of the youngsters.

'And why is that other policeman laughing?' comments another. 'That's not very nice is it?'

A lone voice interjects.

'They're not policemen, they're soldiers. It's a picture about apartheid. The soldiers are chasing the boy because he's black.'

The other children pause for a few moments to think about what the boy has said.

'How do you know that?' asks one of them.

'My brothers told me,' comes the reply.

'Why did they tell you?' asks another.

'So that we can make sure it doesn't happen again. That's what the Truth and Reconciliation Commission is all about.'

11 He hath shewed strength with his arm

I click out of Microsoft Word, shut down the Cathedral Foundation's computer and collect my briefcase.

My second week in Cape Town has nearly passed and I am beginning to find my feet.

The lift takes me down five floors to an Adderley Street which is bathed in late winter sunshine.

'Baas, have your shoe shined,' beckons the suavely-dressed owner of Mr. Tutu's – a street-side shoe-cleaning stand nearby. I am wearing suede boots so his offer – he emphasises each word of it – is singularly inappropriate.

Other offers soon follow.

'Tooee rand...avocados...tooee (it's spelt twee) rand,' a street seller shouts as I saunter on.

'Flowers, Sir. Flowers...twee rand. Buy some nice flowers for the wife, the girlfriend, Sir.'

By now I have reached the turning for the Central Post Office in Cape Town. It teems daily with flower sellers. Glorious flowers – pinks, reds, oranges, yellows, purples. I stop to admire the colourful array before my eyes and then head for the Post Office steps. It is 4.30 p.m. on the dot. I am just in time to catch the post.

I never reach the Post Office however. Instead, four men come bounding towards me. Two snatch at my briefcase. One produces a flick-knife. Another breathes alcohol fumes into my face as he lunges towards me.

'Money, money,' shout the two men who hold one of the handles of my briefcase.

I clutch the other handle less than convincingly.

'Shall I kill him?' the knife-bearer, who is barely sober, asks his fellows.

He raises the knife.

He hath shewed strength with his arm.

I instinctively release the briefcase. As I do so the men pull it away. I stand dazed. I should run but my feet are somehow rooted to the spot. My hand is outstretched as if I am still clutching the bag.

The four men have run off. But seconds later they are back again. They find me still resolutely gazing into thin air.

'It is money Sir?,' grunts the man who is now in possession of my briefcase.

'No, it's religious books,' I reply. Where on earth I produced that line from I shall never know. But without checking the briefcase to verify my story – which is true – the man stretches out one hand to give me back the briefcase and with the other he motions me on my way.

'Sorry, Sir,' he says and rather politely at that.

Has he now shewed strength with his arm?

The following day I consign the briefcase to the back of my wardrobe. It's safer in Cape Town to use a plastic bag.

It is early Spring. Many of South Africa's 'good and great' are gathered one evening in the grounds of the Trauma Centre which is located in what was once District Six.

With stunning vistas of Table Mountain as a backdrop the assembled guests politely sip glasses of wine, enjoy the nibbles and canapés and the trio of youngsters who play Mozart and Haydn.

We have all come for the launch of an important new book. Entitled *Priest and Partisan* it tells the remarkable story of Fr. Michael Lapsley SSM who lost both his hands when, in exile, he received a letter-bomb, since when he has dedicated himself ceaselessly to the cause of healing and reconciliation. Hence his work with those traumatised by their pre-1994 experiences.

Michael now has two metal articulated hooks for hands. Potentially of course this could make the whole business of greeting him difficult. One can hardly shake him by the hand. But such a perception is my problem. It's not one for him. For he greets each of us in a totally natural way by hugging us.

He hath shewed strength with his arm.

I purchase a copy of the book five minutes into the party. This means that I lose my bet with Pat Francis, a friend from the staff of Wola Nani – a Non-Governmental Organisation (NGO) working in the field of HIV/AIDS. I had said to her that I'd last out at least ten minutes before purchasing a copy. But as usual when it comes to books there's no holding me back!

As I queue up to have the book inscribed by Michael my eyes fix on his metal 'hands'. With an amazing degree of precision he uses one metal hook to open the book and hold its cover whilst with the other he deftly manoeuvres his ball-point pen across the title page. He does it all with effortless ease. This surely masks the pain and frustration he must have experienced when a letter-bomb forced him to learn to write in this way?

As my turn comes I am truly transfixed by the signing process. 'Chris, with fond regards, Michael' he writes. As he does so I savour each stroke of his pen. He hath indeed shewed strength with his arm – strength through total weakness.

12 He hath scattered the proud in the imagination of their hearts

Most Wednesday mornings I go to St. George's Grammar School with Christian Hartnick who combines the School's Chaplaincy portfolio with his other duties at the Cathedral. One or other of us or an invited speaker takes the assembly which alternates between the Middle School years and the Seniors and Matrics.

After the assembly we repair to the boarders' dining room for tea and sandwiches. The hour which follows is one of my favourite slots in each week. We both have very similar senses of humour and extremely loud laughs. Previously we were both in the teaching profession and we largely share the same theological interests. Our discussions are always lively and animated.

After a few weeks we agree that they are some of the best discussions we have ever had. Through them we learn a great deal from each other. Invariably they focus on the great mystery which is the Christian Church. But thankfully they are never too 'churchy', for both of us share a conviction that it is high time the Church got its act together in relation to the world. So our musings are always outward-looking in context though inevitably we spend a fair amount of time on the institutional inadequacies of the Church.

What an organisation the Church is! It sets as its goal the eradication of worldly power and hierarchy – that is after all what the gospels teach – but it has nonetheless developed perhaps the most sophisticated hierarchy the world has ever known! The further one moves up this hierarchy the more one also seems to move from enlightenment to ignorance! Which is of course an exaggeration – we know that – but it does contain more than a grain of truth when it comes to some of those right at the top of the tree. So, gleefully, we scatter the proud, the lazy and hypocritical. We dismiss all the schemes they seem to dream up to ensure that the Church remains largely a society for the preservation of the status quo rather than for its removal.

Scattering the proud is an entertaining verbal sport even if it comes from a genuine sense of disappointment and frustration. We give vent to our feelings. But the following Wednesday the proud are still occupying their places in the hierarchy. Doubtless they are up to all their old tricks again as well.

13 He hath put down the mighty from their seat

The Enthronement Service of Archbishop Njongonkulu is a splendid piece of liturgical drama. All the ceremonial which the Anglican Church can muster combines with great pomp and marvellous music to provide as colourful an afternoon as you could ever hope to experience in a church.

For me however the service is somewhat fraught because I have been given the job of dealing with the press! This means that I rarely sit still in one place for more than five minutes as photographers can tend to 'wander' if not closely supervised! I do however make it to my seat as the solemn moment of the enthronement itself approaches.

With due reverence – and with perhaps a sense of the bizarre which Anglicans seem to engineer in very formal worship - Rowan Smith, the Dean, takes the Archbishop by the hand and places him in his throne.

An exhilarating organ fanfare is sounded.

Part of me is greatly moved especially by the vulnerability which is writ large on the Archbishop's face. He seems genuinely daunted by the prospect of his new role. But another part of me is enraged. The Christian Church has done it again. It proclaims a message of good news to the poor and the outcast and yet it enshrines this in such imperialistic rituals.

Originally a bishop sat not in a throne but in his *cathedra* which was merely his teaching seat. What then are we doing placing a bishop – who should be simply a shepherd of sheep, a fellow pilgrim and guide – into a throne which sets him so apart from the rest of us? Why all the trappings of worldly kingship when Christ's rule comes through our ability to get alongside those who need us?

He hath put down the mighty from their seat.

I have a terrible urge to do the same right now. Not because the Archbishop comes across as a high and mighty person but because we are making him into something which seems so far removed from the gospel message of kingship through service.

However, a due sense of Anglican decorum and respect prevents me from wrecking the service by turfing him out of his throne!

I am sitting in the Good Hope Centre on Wednesday 21 August. There is a great sense of anticipation amongst those around me. The Truth and Reconciliation Commission has been hearing submissions from the political parties over the past few days. This morning F.W. de Klerk is to table the National Party's submission. Everyone is wondering what he will say. Will he apologise for the sins of apartheid?

Many of those around me seem to have come in the hope of hearing just such an apology.

'The Nats messed up my whole life,' the person next to me remarks. 'I wanted to be here so that I could tell my grandchildren that I was in the room when they explained their apartheid policy.'

They may do that, I think to myself, but will they apologise?

We are soon to find out as F.W. De Klerk solemnly walks into the room with the Commissioners. We stand for Archbishop Tutu to lead us in prayer and then sit as De Klerk introduces his party's submission.

De Klerk is a highly skilled speaker and as he begins to read the submission he sounds every bit the shrewd lawyer that he is. He sets out the context for the apartheid years methodically and via a lengthy detour into South African history. He narrows it down to the period post 1960 which is the Commission's principal concern.

A group of Nat supporters are enjoying what they hear. Suddenly they erupt in shouts of 'Viva De Klerk!' But Archbishop Tutu is having none of that. Rightly he silences them, reminding us all that we are not attending a political rally! He does so with more than a touch of the school master about him. The Nat supporters, like errant pupils in a class, cower in their seats.

De Klerk resumes his text. Expectations continue to rise. Will he say sorry?

Thumbing through a copy of the submission I see that an apology is imminent. I half read it and am moved by the sentiments it expresses. 'I apologise for all the sufferings caused...' There we have it – the historic apology everyone has been waiting for.

I stop reading and listen to him intone the whole passage. As he does so I realise, much to my disappointment, that my expectations have got the better of me. *The Mail and Guardian*, a weekly newspaper, sums it up aptly in a headline a few days later. 'Ah well...I'm kind of sorry'.

The mighty have fallen from their seats. The apartheid years are over.

De Klerk, perhaps the only politician this century to surrender power voluntarily, even if realistically he did not of course have much choice; De Klerk the Nobel Peace Prize winner; De Klerk the last State President of the apartheid regime, then State Deputy President in the new Government, now Leader of the Opposition; De Klerk, who was once the most influential man in the country but who is now pretty powerless; De Klerk who ended apartheid; this De Klerk nevertheless cannot free himself from his own history as an Afrikaner to see the apartheid years for what they were. For sure he apologises for all the sufferings they caused. But he does so by rationalising the policies he inherited from previous governments as simply a wrong turning taken for the right motives.

The Apartheid leaders have put themselves down from their own seats of Government. That in itself is a remarkable thing. They've lost power but they cannot now lose face. So they trot out the same tedious justifications for their actions which they trotted out during all the years of apartheid.

Jesus asks: what does it profit a man if he gains the whole world and loses his own soul?

I look at F.W. de Klerk and wonder what does it profit a man if he loses the whole world and still seems to be soul-less? Whatever motivated his actions they have certainly profited everyone else. But what does he really think about them deep down, far beneath the rhetoric of De Klerk the professional politician?

14 And hath exalted the humble and meek

The Archbishop moves through the Nave of St. George's on his way to the West Door. His enthronement ordeal – for that is what to an extent it must have been for him – is almost over.

Outside the Cathedral I am just about managing to hold back the press photographers who are determined to obtain their front-page pictures of the new Archbishop blessing the city of Cape Town.

The blessing over, we all move to the Dean's office for the final event of the day – a press conference. The Dean, the Bishop of Natal - who is the senior diocesan bishop after the Primate - and the Archbishop disrobe. Once the visiting clergy have done the same and been ushered out we are on our way.

The press conference should all be very straightforward. The Archbishop's sermon – his Charge – is a major statement of his intentions and vision. In the briefing beforehand I outlined some of the things I thought that the reporters would wish to focus on. True to form they oblige with questions about world debt, education and poverty. But then the Archbishop unexpectedly turns to Ace who is one of the leading journalists of the *Cape Argus*.

'No crunch question from you, Ace?' he asks with a glint in his eye.

'No Njongo', comes the reply. The two men then get up to embrace one another.

For those of us who are mystified by what is all rather irregular behaviour in a press conference, the Archbishop explains that Ace and he have known each other for years since both of them were political prisoners on Robben Island. They continue to greet one another with real affection. It is a touching scene between two men who, in different ways and from humble beginnings, have both reached what a friend of mine calls the 'dizzy heights of excellence'. The suffering which they endured in the apartheid years seems to me transfigured in this radiant human moment which breaks all the tension of a long day. God has indeed exalted the humble and meek.

Despite the improving spring weather of late September, which usually means fewer customers, the Arch is still very busy. It is the cathedral's feeding station for the homeless and, increasingly, for those who come into Cape Town from the townships looking for work.

On Thursdays I dish out soup and bread for a morning and this last Thursday of the month is no exception. As work goes it is not that physically demanding but it is hugely rewarding – a chance to care for the needy in a very practical way and an opportunity to give them a sense of the dignity and respect which they deserve. Simply saying 'What can I do for you, Sir' or 'Madam' can make a small but not insignificant contribution to the process. Not many people after all address vagrants as Sir or Madam.

We open at 9 a.m. The queues keep us busy on this particular Thursday for a couple of hours. Then Themba appears clutching a small green chit. He has been working at the craft table where Coke cans are transformed into beautiful candleholders. The green chit which he is about to present to me means that he has made a holder and is thus entitled to a free cup of soup and some bread. This is known as a 'special' and normally costs thirty cents. As he gives me the chit he can hardly restrain the smile of pride and excitement which is waiting to break out all over his face. Momentarily Themba's shattered self-worth is restored. A truly humble man is exalted and exhilarated.

Domine Herbie Brandt arrives at the Cathedral to lead a time of prayer and meditation in an Inter-faith Day of Prayer and Fasting which Vivien Harber and I have co-ordinated. It is a response to the ongoing violence between PAGAD (People Against Gangsterism and Drugs) and the gangsters, violence which is creating immense tension throughout the City but especially amongst the township communities on the Cape Flats. The Vigil lasts from 7 a.m. to 7 p.m. It includes prayers lead by Roman Catholic and Anglican priests, Orthodox and Reformed rabbis, a Muslim Moulana and an Imam, a Hindu Guru, members of the Sufi movement, Buddhists and a group from the local Yoga Centre. It is quite a gathering and people approach their prayers or meditations in widely differing ways.

Each person or group has been asked to bring a symbol of their religious tradition as a focus for their hour of prayer. Domine Brandt has brought a Bible - which is no surprise as he's from the Reformed Christian tradition. Its presence brings out all the worst kind of religious prejudice in me. Doubtless he will offer us a wordy prayer or two as well - as that seems to go hand in hand with those who don't ever put the Good Book down. Sure enough, within moments, my prejudices are confirmed. His prayer is indeed very wordy. But as I listen I feel more and more ashamed of myself. For the words he uses are strikingly beautiful and evocative – a real plea from the heart. His style and manner points to a man who truly knows God. I am forced to face my appalling arrogance which contrasts so sharply with a Domine who radiates such humility. He hasn't brought the 'answers' as I wrongly suspected he would. Rather he simply asks of God the right 'questions' as should all theology and prayer. Would that I had the wisdom and the humility to do the same.

Some weeks before the Archbishop's enthronement I arrive at the Yizani Centre with a request. Those of us on the organising committee would like to have an illustration of the Cathedral done by a street-child for the order of service. This would be especially apposite as one of the Archbishop's most urgent concerns is the plight of the poor both locally and internationally. Juliet Ventor, who co-ordinates the art programme, responds with enthusiasm and a week later I return to help her judge the competition which she has organised amongst the Yizani boys. The standard is very high and we find it difficult to select one picture from amongst so many good ones. Eventually we choose a beautiful picture by Sipho Booysen which is duly reproduced on the inside cover of the order of service. Needless to say he is extremely pleased both then and a few days after the enthronement when we give him a copy of the finished product signed by the Archbishop.

'Why don't we have an exhibition at the Cathedral,' I suggest to Juliet, who is a bit daunted at first by another request but who agrees that it would be a splendid idea. So we fix some dates and over the next few weeks we assemble a huge array of material for display.

As the time comes for the exhibition itself we discuss how best both to publicise it – we host a preview for Cape Town worthies! – and how to ensure that the Yizani boys actually see their work. This will need careful thought so that we do not upset the sensibilities of some people who do not respond too positively to the presence of street children in their midst! We decide that we ourselves will take them to the Cathedral on a couple of occasions, to one of which we will invite the press. Central to the exhibition is some work by Sipho who is very gifted artistically. But a few days before we open Sipho is nowhere to be found. He doesn't seem to be coming to the Drop-in Centre and no one seems to have seen him on the streets either. We are concerned for his welfare and disappointed that he may not get to see his work on view. But we have to open so we go ahead as planned.

By chance, on the third day of the exhibition, I spot Sipho wandering down Government Avenue next to the Cathedral. I am heading in the opposite direction but I decide that I must nonetheless take the chance to show him the exhibition. So I head towards him and invite him to come with me. He gladly agrees. Indeed he is quite excited at the prospect of seeing his artwork in such a grand setting.

Just outside the cathedral I am waylaid by some needy street-people. They want money – which I tend not to give them – so instead I offer to buy them some food. I send Sipho on ahead of me into the Cathedral, explaining to him where his artwork is located, whilst I head to a nearby sandwich bar.

About five minutes later I return to find Sipho in tears on the Cathedral steps.

'What on earth is wrong?' I ask.

'Man tell me...get out,' he says.

And in an instant I know what has happened. Because Sipho has come into the cathedral unaccompanied he has been sent packing. Of course it's my fault because it had been agreed that the Yizani boys should not come into the exhibition without supervision from their carers. I understand the reasoning behind this. But I am fed up nonetheless. For what does it say about our ministry as Christians if we can embrace Sipho's artistic but not his actual presence amongst us?

A few days after our encounter in the Arch I bump into Themba on Cape Town's Grand Parade. I stop to chat to him. But his facial expression is totally different. Now there is a look of despondency about him.

'No work, Baas,' he says to me. He repeats the phrase with total resignation in his voice.

In the Arch last Thursday Themba had fleetingly experienced a real sense of exaltation. Now all that is gone.

15 He hath filled the hungry with good things

In mid-September Wola Nani jointly stages a conference with the CPSA to consider issues for church leaders arising from the HIV/AIDS pandemic. Speakers come from the United States of America, New Zealand and the United Kingdom as well as from South Africa itself.

The opening of the conference takes a fairly standard format. The delegates register and together with other guests enjoy a glass or two of Cape wine accompanied by some delightfully moreish snacks. Church functions are invariably marked by such receptions, which are without doubt one of the great attractions of the Christian Church! This one is no exception.

Whilst the visiting speakers introduce the themes of the conference Vivien and I, who have both been busy registering the delegates, start to clear up the debris from the reception. There is quite a lot of food left over. What are we going to do with it? We decide to take it to the street people on the Grand Parade or in Long Street, or to those who sleep in the cathedral's North Porch. The snacks have been served on colourfully-arranged silver platters. So we fill one of these with the leftovers and put it in Vivien's car.

The ceremonies concluded we speed off to the centre of Cape Town in search of street people. We haven't travelled very far when we both hear the platter slide and crash against the rear window and fall all over the boot.

'Damn,' we say in unison.

Vivien stops the car and I get out to inspect the damage.

'It's just so difficult having a social conscience,' I inform Vivien as I try to manoeuvre most of the food back on to the platter – at which we both fall helplessly about with laughter.

I close the boot, the back of which is smeared with avocado puree. I decide that I must sit with the platter in the front of the car.

We reach town and to our surprise the Grand Parade is largely deserted as is Long Street. Eventually we find a couple dozing in the North Porch of St. George's. So out I hop, platter in hand, to dispense dainty little canapés – or what's left of them – to the needy. What a ridiculous scene! How eccentric I must look to the couple in the porch and to the three or four passers-by. I am unperturbed by this however. I am just pleased that someone has benefited from the leftovers.

We have filled the hungry, and certainly we have given them good things to eat.

It's a hard life indeed having a social conscience. All those avocado smears. It'll take ages to clean the car boot. What a pain!

One Sunday afternoon I queue for a couple of hours to take the cable-car to the top of Table Mountain. It is well worth the wait. The panoramic view of the City Bowl and of Table Bay is unbelievably captivating. The memory of it will certainly stay with me for the rest of my life. But I wonder if the memory of all those vagrants and street people, far below me now, will be as strong? In the years to come will I remember them daily tugging at my conscience as they plead:

'Uncle, uncle, please give us fifty cents for some bread?'

After a Friday night choir rehearsal in August I return to my flat in Rondebosch to find that there is next to nothing in the larder for supper – not even a can of baked beans. I root around and eventually come up with half a loaf of stale bread. Perhaps now I know what life is like for so many Capetonians? But that isn't of course true at all. I can nip round the corner to a Pizza place and afford the luxury of a meal out whilst they still root around in bins for stale bread which, in desperation, they will probably eat.

The first time I am asked to preach at St. George's I immediately encounter the challenges and constraints which any lectionary of readings imposes on a preacher. Those set for Evensong are the 'Rape of Tamar' in First Samuel and the 'Stilling of the Storm' in Mark's Gospel.

Rarely one to dodge a difficult intellectual challenge however, I use Tamar's rape as a way into talking about 'abuse' in modern societies and especially abusive relationships within families. For it is such abuse which has led so many children to flee their homes and to seek refuge on the streets of Cape Town. Tragically for them they unwittingly replace one form of abuse with others –

drugs, thinners, alcohol, glue and prostitution – to name but a few.

I connect this – deftly I think – with the Sunday-school interpretation of the 'Stilling of the Storm'. This would have us all believe that the Church is the boat and the world is the sea. The boat is thus the place to be if we wish to avoid the storms of life. And of course the Church can be a safe haven in the storm. But, as I point out, if those in the Church really want to change the world, as they say they do, then they will simply have to jump overboard and immerse themselves in the sea itself. Or at least they will have to get alongside those who are stranded on the quayside – those who haven't yet made it into the boat and who may have no wish to do so. They will have to meet people like the children who live in the cathedral's North Porch – on the quayside between St. George's and the World outside – where they are.

The following morning I arrive at the cathedral for the 7.15 a.m. Mass feeling very tired – too tired really to pray properly. What I need is just to 'sit' in the liturgy, to let it carry me along and to soak up its rhythmic familiarity. During the Intercessions other rhythms intrude upon the calmness of the Eucharist thus far! Very loud pop music strikes up making it impossible to hear Chris Ahrends' voice at all. It comes from a street child's ghetto blaster and echoes deafeningly around the North Porch – which is next to St. John's Chapel where the Eucharist is being celebrated.

The noise certainly wakes me out of my liturgical slumber and it makes me feel very irritable. All I had wanted to do this morning was to start the day with some peace and quiet. I have forgotten my words of the previous evening.

'The needs of the world are always pressing in on the Church to shatter the calm complacency of religious serenity.'

An uplifting phrase indeed. I'm rather proud of it. But if only those needs didn't have to intrude on my life at half-past seven on a Monday morning.

16 And the rich he hath sent empty away

'Sir, I am from Durban. Have no fear. I am a Zulu. I am a Christian. I have been looking for work. I have just got a job this morning. It starts tomorrow. But I have a wife and four children. Sir, I need money to feed them today. Please can you help me?'

The crisply rehearsed phrases of this Zulu man confront me in St. George's Mall on six or seven separate occasions. Sometimes the number of children changes but the request is always the same! My Zulu friend never remembers that I've heard this speech from him so many times before. He never bothers to change his story. Clearly he is lying. I don't give him a cent. Sometimes I don't even bother to direct him to the Arch where he would be given food because I find him extremely tiresome.

My response to him is greatly hampered by his untruthfulness. He isn't rich but he isn't destitute either. So I can send him away empty-handed and not feel too much of a conscience about his situation. But each time I meet him a nagging feeling lurks at the back of my mind. What if one day his request were to be genuine? What if he were then to be very much in need? I wouldn't be able to tell whether he was being honest or not because he's destroyed any potential trust I might have in what he says. For sure I will send him away empty-handed as I have done before. But perhaps I might then be dispatching a poor man from my presence without helping him at all.

That thought preys on my conscience, for the *Magnificat* demands that the rich be sent away empty-handed, not the poor.

'Sir, I am from Durban. Have no fear. I am a Zulu. I am a Christian. I have been looking for work. I have just got a job this morning. It starts tomorrow. But I have a wife and four children. Sir, I need money to feed them today. Please can you help me?'

17 He remembering his mercy hath holpen his servant Israel

I am preaching in St. George's Cathedral one Sunday morning in September. The gospel reading is the Parable of the Labourers in the Vineyard. I use the parable as a way into discussing the anti-Semitism which is to be found in the Gospels. I do so by focusing on the phrase with which the parable begins and ends – 'so the last will be first and the first will be last'. I try to show that for Matthew the 'last' were the followers of Christ and the 'first' were the Jews. I go on to examine some of the appalling effects which such a theology of rejection has had on the Church's treatment of its Jewish sisters and brothers.

As I preach I feel that I am doing my bit, albeit in a small way, to help God's servant Israel. I'm also trying to help the self-understanding of Christians. My hope is that if we can be reconciled to the truth of our own religious past we may be able to move out more meaningfully into a world crying out for its brokenness to be healed. It is a sermon which conflates long-term issues of Jewish-Christian relations with pressing issues of truth and reconciliation in South Africa.

I deliver the sermon with a confidence which comes from my passionate engagement with both subjects. But it is a confidence which belies the huge doubts I have in my head as to how rounded a picture I am actually painting. As I speak I cannot erase from my mind the awful images which I have seen in recent television coverage of the Israeli-Palestinian situation. I know that I am right to point out that Christians have oppressed and still do oppress Jews. But what about the way in which the Jews themselves, oppressed for so long, have become oppressors of others? Are not the Palestinians God's children too? Shouldn't I also be helping their cause as I preach?

After the launch of the Children's Ubuntu Project at the end of October I go on leave for a couple of weeks. I spend a week in Johannesburg as the guest of the Community of the Resurrection and then I travel to Durban where my host is Rodney Harber, a leading town-planner. On my second day I take a train to nearby Pietermaritzburg. I arrive at the station onto which Gandhi was famously ejected from a 'whites only' carriage. I head into the city and visit its modern anglican cathedral before entering the Church of the Vow. It is here that I touch base with the heart of Afrikaner nationalism.

Over the previous months I have tried to understand something of Afrikaner history. One of the things which has most struck me is the way in which biblical imagery – especially imagery from the Hebrew Bible – has been grafted onto a narrative in which Afrikaners have seen themselves not only as God's elect but also as the new Israel. Hence the Great Trek was really a re-run of the Exodus narrative – the means by which Afrikaners claimed the Promised Land for themselves and made a covenant with God as his chosen people.

So I stand in the Church of the Vow surrounded by just such covenantal imagery. As I do so I cannot help but ponder the appalling consequences of such a world-view in the wickedness of apartheid which came from it.

Why is it, I ask myself, that groups of human beings – especially self-proclaimed religious groupings – seem always to claim preferential relationships with God? Surely God himself does not promise to help one group as opposed to another? So why treat him as if he did?

I leave the building wondering if there is not in fact something inherently wicked in religion itself. If it can give rise to such evil – as it so often has in crusades or inquisitions or pogroms – hadn't we all better do without it?

The cathedral choir and clergy move in procession from the stalls towards the vestry. It is Christmas Eve and the Festival of Nine Lessons and Carols is reaching its climax with the hymn *Hark the herald angels sing.* As we turn the corner and move down the steps at the crossing I catch a glimpse out of the corner of my eye of Imam Rashied with some members of his Mosque congregation. He has asked to come to this Christmas service as he wishes to celebrate and pray with us at one of our most holy seasons. So it is that I see and hear him greeting, as lustily as anyone else in the packed cathedral, Christ the 'new-born King'. And as I do so many of the questions which I have agonised over in the past few months dissolve before me. There is hope for the world after all when the adherents of one religion are prepared, with such generosity, to enter into the experience and beliefs of another.

18 As he promised to our forefathers, Abraham and his seed, for ever

One event of great sadness mars the Inter-faith Day of Prayer and Fasting for Peace which is held at St. George's on the last day of August. We have asked children from three schools to bring pictures, prayers and poems for peace during the morning. St. Cyprian's School, an Anglican foundation, arrives first. Next comes the Rahmaniyeh Institute, a Muslim School. Finally the Weizmann School, a Jewish foundation, arrives. A Rabbi from the Reformed tradition is leading prayers as they do so. Muslim children sit at his feet. A more powerful expression of inter-faith co-operation I cannot imagine. The Rabbi invites the Muslim children to read some of their own prayers. There is a sense of shared worship in what follows. It moves everyone there.

I go to the doors of the Cathedral to greet the children from the Weizmann School together with their teacher. I beckon them inside. But the teacher says that they are not allowed to enter. Why, I wonder? It transpires that there are two problems. For one thing these Orthodox Jewish children are only allowed inside a Church when it is not being used for prayer. For another the prayers are being lead by a rabbi who is not from their own tradition. This is a scenario which we had not foreseen at the planning stages of the day.

I can see that the children are itching to come inside the building but they are not allowed to do so. They press themselves as close to the glass doors as possible. But that is as close as they are going to get.

Theologically speaking, two things fundamentally unite Muslims, Jews and Christians – they all believe that God is one and they all trace a common lineage from Abraham. An increasing awareness of this has in recent years enabled the three communities to undertake all sorts of joint initiatives. Such joint action was a big feature of the struggle against apartheid especially in the 1980s. In my own country the thought of Muslims, Jews and Christians praying together would appear to be too radical a concept for a people with largely 'conservative' sensibilities – it doesn't happen very often. In South Africa it has gone on for years.

Early on in 1996 I visited Jerusalem. Ostensibly I went to do some research work into Christian and Jewish responses to the Holocaust or the Shoah. But whilst I was there I had inevitably to 'do' all the holy sights. For Christians most of these are to be found in the 'Old' City. With its various religious 'Quarters' it is a colourful place bursting with activity. It is however a baffling place for any pilgrim. The Via Dolorosa is horrifically commercialised. The churches – whose use is often divided between different Christian groups largely at war with one another – are hardly very prayerful. The mosques however tell a different story. It was in the Dome of the Rock that I found almost the only haven of peace and tranquillity on offer. So I spent several hours on consecutive days praying there near the rock on which, it is said, Abraham so nearly sacrificed Isaac. Ironically it was there that I felt closest to the reality of a God who had, I believe, once trodden the sacred temple pavements on which the Dome was later built.

In South Africa, I have been fortunate to work in a Cathedral which is truly prayerful. St. George's is a beautiful building which possesses fabulously rich stained glass, mostly by the French artist Gabriel Loire. These windows are wonderful treasures. Many are the hours I have spent simply focusing my attention on one or other of them. By contrast my attendance at daily Mass has been somewhat sporadic. I have kept to a strict discipline of remembering my family and friends each day by lighting candles in front of the African Madonna near the entrance to St. John's Chapel. I have spent at least half an hour in the building praying or meditating each day and I've kept up with the saying of the Daily Offices in the office or on the Metro or wherever I happened to be when it was time to recite them. I feel as if I have been praying the Offices very much in the world. But I haven't been especially drawn to the rhythm of daily Mass. I think that's partly due to the fact that Christian worship is often so wordy.

The English novelist E.M. Forster used to refer to 'poor little talkative Christianity'. I share his sentiments. Early in the morning I just can't cope with all the words one must get through in the Mass. I prefer to 'be' before God rather than to be 'doing' too much 'God-talk' – at least at 7.15 a.m.! By lunchtime I have usually warmed to the task a little better. But even so I have often found that when you work so close to a great building you often need alternative spaces in which to pray and to think through things with a wider sense of perspective. I have found the Claremont Main Road Mosque to be such a space.

I am sure that Imam Rashied Omar would not mind my saying that the Claremont Mosque cannot compare architecturally with the Dome of the Rock or with St. George's Cathedral for that matter. But architecture does not make a place prayerful. What makes it prayerful is the rhythm of those praying within it who allow God to use them to sustain it as a temple of the holy. The Claremont Mosque has clearly been nourished in this way. It has been my great privilege to share in the worship of its community.

My experience in the Claremont Mosque has powerfully reminded me of a sermon text I recall from my chorister days.

'The truth which holds us, is always greater than the truth we hold to'.

So said John Tinsley the Bishop of Bristol at the time.

What prophetic words indeed. For the promises which sustain all the children of Abraham are surely always much greater than the commitments and promises to which individual children hold? At the Claremont Mosque this truth has become a reality for me. I have learnt that unity in diversity is possible. It does not mean surrendering one's differences in the hope of finding a common ground for belief. We all need the particularities of our faith traditions. But surely it does mean that we can surrender the arrogance of our claims to universality?

Isn't it in fact about time we stopped pretending that the tradition to which we belong tells the whole truth and nothing but the truth? Can't we all come to God through our own particularity without universalising this experience?

19 Glory be to the Father, and to the Son: and to the Holy Ghost

Fr. Rowan Smith is installed as the fourteenth Dean of Cape Town in the context of Festal Evensong on the Feast of St. Edward the Confessor. The Christian community celebrates its sense of self-identity in style. It recommits itself to be a baptismal, biblically based, Eucharistic and prayerful people, witnessing to its belief in God as Father, Son and Holy Ghost. No one could leave the building in any doubt about that!

A few days before the service Imam Rashied Omar speaks to me about his involvement. He is to read a greeting to the new Dean together with Jewish and Hindu colleagues. He is also bringing some members of his Mosque community with him.

'Normally,' he tells me, 'we pray at 7.00 p.m.'

The Installation starts at 6.00p.m. and will not be over by then.

'We can delay our prayers until 7.30 p.m. But if we do so, is there anywhere we can go quietly to pray before joining the reception after the service?'

'Of course,' I reply.

We set aside space in St. John's Chapel where the Muslims can pray.

The Installation is rich in symbolism but I find the most powerful symbol of all to be that of Rashied and his fellow Muslims at prayer in the Cathedral.

The Children of Abraham pray together in one place. If that doesn't give glory to Father, Son and Holy Spirit I don't know what would.

20 As it was in the beginning, is now, and ever shall be: world without end

Whenever I visit a foreign country I like if possible to visit its Parliament. It is always interesting to see how a country reflects its sense of identity in the art, architecture and general 'feel' of its central institutions. I anticipate in this regard that the South African Parliament will be in a state of transition between the use of its buildings by the 'old' regime and their redeployment by the 'new'. My expectations are not disappointed when I pitch up at the Parliament buildings during my first week in Cape Town.

I enter the buildings to notice instantly that colonial grandeur jostles uneasily with a United Nations sponsored exhibition of anti-apartheid art works. I quickly reach the tours desk but find that some of the guides are on holiday. I am asked if I would therefore mind joining a group of sixty children from one of the township schools for a tour. I don't mind in the least. In fact I am delighted to do so as I believe that you learn most about a country the more time you spend with its children.

As we walk around the corridors of power and visit the impressive chambers I strike up a good rapport with the children. They quickly find out that I am British and consequently they ask me lots of questions about the Royal Family. The many portraits of British Royals which cover the walls of the Parliament buildings and other telltale signs of a colonial past have partly prompted these no doubt. And they make me feel somewhat uneasy because they represent a history of oppression about which I am embarrassed. I had similar feelings when I visited the Victoria Monument in Calcutta, India. It also is jam-packed with colonial artefacts.

As it was in the beginning it ever would be. That must have been the hope of those who built the British Empire. World without end.

I remember all the pink on the rather out-dated map of the world which was hung on the wall of my very first classroom at school. I blush a darker shade of pink at the shame of the Empire. Thank God that it came to an end.

The Parliamentary Tour is given by an immensely charming, informative and enthusiastic university student from Khayalitscha. It reaches its climax in the newest chamber which was built in P.W. Botha's time to encompass the 'coloured' assembly he inaugurated as a 'reform' of the apartheid system. Now it is where all the Members of Parliament in the Government of National Unity have their seats. The children file in in awed silence.

'Is this really where Madiba sits?' a little girl of ten asks me with a look of excited anticipation in her face.

Before I have time to say that I'm not sure the Guide begins to address us.

'Over there is where the President sits,' he informs us and all the children lunge in the direction to which he is pointing in order to get a view of the place where their hero sits.

The children are allowed to wander round. They delight in touching the leather of the seats and the beautiful wood which fills the chamber. Maxishe, a very chatty thirteen-year-old boy, who has kept me entertained with his perceptive, witty and articulate comments throughout the tour, gazes around the chamber. He turns to me with real pride and proclaims:

'This is ours now. No one can ever take it away from us.'

I feel a lump in my throat...Out of the mouth of babes...I do hope that he's right...World without end.

21 Amen

Over the past two years of my ordination training I have often discussed two of my greatest passions – music and sport – with Michael, a fellow ordinand from the United States of America. He is now back in Chicago completing his training.

Our conversations have been mutually enriching. I miss them very much. In one of them I remember Mike pointing out that a great sporting occasion can encapsulate the whole narrative of a nation's history, hopes and aspirations. This profound insight has helped me to understand much better the treasure-trove of sporting memories which I carry around with me.

The first Friday of July 1977 is a day which will for ever be emblazoned on my memory. I was almost ten years old and watching Britain's Virginia Wade battle it out against Holland's Betty Stove for the Wimbledon Ladies Singles Trophy. To reach this moment those of us who follow tennis had been on a very long journey with Miss Wade. There had been many near misses and a great deal of heartache. But now a British woman was in a Wimbledon final for the first time in ages. It was Silver Jubilee year. The Queen was making one of her rare visits to the Championships that same afternoon. Glorious sunshine bathed the hallowed turf of the Centre Court. A sea of Union Jacks waved at every opportunity. National hopes – I daresay supported by a few prayers – were pinned on 'Our Ginny'.

She started tentatively – as she often did – losing the first set. The crowd's groans were audible. But slowly she began to drag herself back into the match. Battling bravely she levelled the match at one set all. She adopted a 'chip and charge' approach in the final set, risking everything for the chance to hold the golden trophy of her dreams. She brought herself to match point with some very fierce driving down the lines. The Centre Court was as silent as I've ever known it to be.

Betty Stove tossed the ball in the air. The serve was rather short. Virginia Wade unleashed a fine, low, forehand return. Stove was quickly at the net, prepared for the first volley she would have to play. But the return was too powerful and wide – it was perfect.

A whole nation, avidly watching its television sets, gasped in relief. 'Our Ginny' had done it. The Centre Court erupted to the strains of 'For she's a jolly good fellow'. It was an unforgettable sound. The nation had broken into song. Its hopes – and prayers – had come together in one moment of pure joy.

I followed the 1995 Rugby World Cup with great interest. It seemed to me that most of the rest of the globe did the same. When South Africa reached the final a group of us got together for a party in the hope that we would see the 'rainbow nation' pull off what would be a memorable victory against the New Zealand All Blacks.

Television coverage fully captured the drama of a nation's story played out in eighty minutes of rugby. We all looked on in eager anticipation of the expected 'happy ending'. And a world short of good news received a headline story never to be forgotten. Moving images of Madiba in a Springbok jersey, of Pianaar with the trophy and of De Klerk, as animated as his somewhat formal personality allows him to be, were flashed around the globe.

Years of struggle and strife had been transfigured into ecstatic joy. The Springboks had brought dream to reality. The 'rainbow nation' had given the whole world a song to sing.

When I arrived in South Africa I was determined to watch some top-class rugby. Luckily for me, living in Rondebosch for much of the time, Norwich Park, Newlands was but a stone's throw away on the Metro.

Early on in my stay my former charges from King's College Choir in Cambridge visited Cape Town on their first South African tour. Soon after, the Springboks were due to play the All Blacks again. The South African public awaited a re-match of the 1995 World Cup Final with eager anticipation. Alastair Hussain, the Senior Chorister at King's, had stayed on in Cape Town for a holiday with his parents Nor and Rosemary and his brother Leo, who had also been a chorister during my time at King's. Like me Alastair had followed the World Cup with great interest. I had of course supported England until they were knocked out in the semi-finals. But Alastair had supported the Springboks from the start. Knowing his love of rugby I booked some standing tickets for all of us to go to the Newlands test. I also took along Ivan, the young son of Barry Smith's housekeeper, Sophie – Ivan being another avid rugby supporter.

I have been to many international matches at Twickenham but the atmosphere of a Newlands test is something else! The crowd of people around us was wonderfully relaxed, friendly and welcoming. Their flag-waving, joking and cheering made for a splendid afternoon's entertainment. It was the New South Africa at its very best.

In the first half the Springboks played some of the best running rugby you could ever hope to see. The quality of the passing was phenomenal. The overlapping and second-phase play was of the highest order. At half time the crowd had much to sing about. The South Africans were well on top of things. But the second half told a different story. It saw the All Blacks up the tempo and the level of their play. We all watched in disbelief as they literally walked off with the match.

The crowd's mood was inevitably more downbeat at the end. But there were three or four tests to go and the South Africans had at least proved in the first half that they could still live at the highest levels of the game. So all was not lost.

It seemed to me however that a national narrative of a somewhat different sort had been played out in the eighty minutes of play which we had watched. The 'rainbow nation' had shown that it could still sing the song of triumph which had reverberated around the globe in April 1994 and July 1995. But as it settled down to the business of willing a fledgling democracy into sustainable life it was hitting struggles of a new kind. The foundation voice, the cantus firmus of the Rainbow Song, was as strong as ever. But around it the other voices were not always sounding concordantly. At times indeed they seemed to be echoing the melodies of other songs, of other narratives altogether.

Two weeks before I arrived in Cape Town my favourite fourteen days of the year began – Wimbledon fortnight!

Early on in the tournament a handsome and charming young man, a Briton – no less – from rural Oxfordshire, created a sensation. We all knew that Tim Henman had the game for grass. We also knew that he had a great temperament as well. But we didn't know whether he could make it all come together at Wimbledon. In his first round match he played the Russian Yevgeny Kafelnikov who was seeded five. It was one of the most aesthetically pleasing tennis matches I have ever seen. Both players were at the top of their form. The groundstrokes were beautifully executed. The volleying was crisp and sharp. The two men served powerfully and accurately. After five epic sets Henman emerged on top. The crowd was ecstatic. We were all back in 1977 again! A nation without many tennis stars to root for of late now most certainly had a player to take on the best in the world. And the thing which made Tim so appealing was his great modesty. He brushed off relentless press coverage and national expectations with a shrug of the shoulders. He would simply do what he could do best, namely, play tennis. Everyone else could get all hyped-up with excitement. He'd just get on with the job.

As the tournament progressed I became more and more animated! Henman secured victory after victory and found himself in the quarter-finals. A British man had not been so far at Wimbledon since 1973! The nation went wild – as did the press. Might we actually be watching this year's champion? It was not a totally unrealistic prospect as so many seeds had been knocked out of the draw. If Tim could get past America's Todd Martin there was no knowing what he might be able to achieve!

Sadly it was not to be. Tim never really got going in a match much interrupted by showers and he lost in straight sets. The newspapers turned their attention to other stories. Tim Henman went back to rural Oxfordshire for a holiday. But on the streets of Britain a new hero had been born. Municipal courts were by all accounts booked up for weeks afterwards as enthusiastic amateurs retrieved their dusty racquets from the lofts into which they had been consigned. The talk was all of the rising star, Tim Henman. Might Britain at last have produced a man capable of lifting the Men's Singles trophy?

Great pieces of music, like great sporting occasions, tell their stories. They have definite beginnings and endings – often with substantial musical journeys in between. The grammar of music is such that its very essence is departure and return. A movement from a classical symphony begins with melodic and harmonic material which will at length be restated – though it will have been transformed considerably by then. In between, an endless series of conflicts and resolutions jostle with one another to define a musical journey. This musical process is of course very much like life itself. We may not be terribly good at conflict-resolution but our attempts dominate the fabric of our lives nonetheless. They provide a counterpoint or commentary which defines the stories we try to narrate and the courses we chart for ourselves.

Sometimes, as in Beethoven's *Ninth Symphony*, the musical journey is so long and so complex that when we hear the 'Ode to Joy' bringing the work to a climax we think that we have reached new territory – that we have found the real song to sing. But in actual fact the content of Beethoven's 'Ode to Joy' is all implicit in what has happened before across the symphony. It is to be found in the tightly-knit fabric of tension and resolution which propels the music on its way.

When we reach the conclusion of our life's work and, through the grace of God, we enter into the fullness of his kingdom we might similarly be tempted to believe that we are standing on new, holy ground. But as with Beethoven's *Ode to Joy*, so with our entrance into heaven. For the whole meaning of the Incarnation lies in a belief that the kingdom of God breaks into this world through Jesus Christ. The angels sing over Bethlehem. They trumpet a new world order. The kingdom is thus already here. This cantus firmus may become lost in a maze of counter-melodies but it remains the foundation voice of our life's song, whatever material with which we choose to surround it. So when we walk through the gates of heaven we should hear the strains of a familiar song. We should feel a sense of return. We will have arrived where we started. The music of our lives will have been transformed. It will have transformed us too. But there will be an underlying continuity to the main theme.

The best liturgy takes people where they are, gathers together their gifts and uses these to point beyond itself to the reality of a God whose kingdom is pressing in on this world all the time. Music is often the means through which the very best of this world is offered to God. But great though such musical liturgy may be, it is only ever a foretaste of heaven. It is the 'Adagio' before the much expected 'Allegro'. It is an echo of a place in which there will be 'no noise nor silence, but one equal music', to use John Donne's evocative phrase.

Despite what many contemporary Christian theologians tell us, the kingdom of God is not co-extensive with this world. We Christians are not it! We are caught up in the kingdom. We are the body of Christ. But we await full transformation into Christ-likeness. This is an on-going process. We certainly sing the melody of the kingdom song and our singing points the way forward. But the harmonic structure on which this melody hangs is in a process of constant evolution. What the world hears is an echo of a song yet fully to be realised.

It is my turn to chant the Office of Evensong when we celebrate the Feast of St. Michael and All Angels at St. George's Cathedral.

During the service the Choir leads us in the singing of one of my favourite hymns – *Angel-voices ever singing*. I've never been too sure what to think about angels, so Vivien Harber's sermon helps me a great deal. For she argues that she has gained a sense of what angels might be like through the graciousness and resilience of the abused children with whom she has worked. Through them she has heard the message of the angels. It is a message of hope amidst suffering. I could not agree more with her. This has been my experience too.

I bear all that in mind as I join with the choir in singing the hymn. I thank God for all the children with whom I have worked and through whom I have heard echoes of the divine message of salvation. We reach verse four which has always meant a great deal to me because from childhood it has helped me to make sense of the musical dimension in my life:

> Yea, we know that thou rejoicest
> o'er each work of thine;
> thou didst ears and hands and voices
> for thy praise design;
> craftman's art and music's measure
> for thy pleasure
> all combine.

I don't know how pleasurable the Lord finds our singing of the verse but, as we reach its fifth line and I look at the choir, I am overwhelmed with emotion.

There is a special poignancy about the singing for me because this choir is a multi-racial one. Long before 1994 Barry Smith, the choir's Director, had ensured that, at least in God's house, all God's people would sing his praises together.

I pause to reflect on the story of all those years of struggle against a vicious and cruel system. I also think of the heartache and struggle which the running of such a choir must have involved for Barry, who has not had the luxury of the Choir School set-ups it has been my great privilege to enjoy.

I thank God for his hard work and for the service that generations of choir members have given in God's name.

I thank God for the fact that this choir was a symbol of the way things could be through those terrible years of apartheid.

I ask God to help us to remember their immense but perhaps largely unsung contribution to the anti-apartheid movement in South Africa. For a tradition as unique and precious as this one, a tradition which by its very existence narrated a story which only now is everyone's for the taking, could so easily be taken for granted.

Like a rainbow in the sky, whose presence is only ever a transitory thing, it could easily disappear if it is not cherished and appreciated.

I look at the faces of the choir members, of every colour and race. As I do so I know that through their singing I am enjoying a foretaste of the kingdom.

I am hearing echoes of a rainbow song. Amen.